# THE
# FIDO
## FACTOR

## How to Get a Leg Up at Work

By Krissi & Dan Barr

D1445264

*The Fido Factor* by Krissi & Dan Barr,
published by Barr Corporate Success

Copyright © 2017 by Krissi Barr and Dan Barr

Printed in the United States of America

First printing, 2017
ISBN 978-0-9991656-0-7

Barr Corporate Success
1319 Parkridge Place
Cincinnati, OH 45208

www.KrissiBarr.com

For information about special discounts available for bulk purchases, sales promotions, fund-raising and educational needs, contact the publisher at the address above.

Illustrations by Gerry Pasqualetti
Layout by Stephen Sullivan and Gerry Pasqualetti
Printed by CJ Krehbiel

**For dogs everywhere and the love
and lessons they've given us.**

# Praise for *The Fido Factor*

*Don't be fooled by the cuddly premise –* FIDO *is a clever toolkit full of thoughtful leadership advice. Enjoyable as it is practical, this book is a great addition to any dog-loving executive's reading list.*
**– Billy Cyr, CEO, Freshpet**

The Fido Factor *is a must-read for anyone who is or wants to be a leader. If you happen to be a dog lover, you do not want to miss this book!*
**– Marshall Goldsmith, #1 Leadership Thinker in the World (Thinkers 50) and best-selling author of** *What Got You Here Won't Get You There, Mojo* **and** *Triggers*

*The unexpected combination of dogs and business leadership makes this one of the most enjoyable — and insightful — books I've read in a long time.*
**– Scott Farmer, CEO, Cintas**

*There is no greater honor than to have others allowing you the opportunity to lead from behind! In* The Fido Factor *both Dan & Krissi have provided us numerous examples & real life chances to actually do it! Well, well done!*
**– Sheldon Yellen, CEO, BELFOR**

*They say you can't teach an old dog new tricks. Sometimes you don't need to.* The Fido Factor *focuses on tried and true leadership concepts and fundamentals for the authentic leader. It contains a blend of insight, humor, old dog "tales" and practicality to make for a quick read for aspiring and proven leaders alike.*
**– Tony Kuczinski, President & CEO, Munich Reinsurance America**

*Leadership lessons from dogs? Woof yes! Like a game seven walk-off homer,* The Fido Factor *shows how to lead your entire team to victory.*
**– Thom Brennaman, SPCA Cincinnati Board Member and Sportscaster**

*Like a Chihuahua, I recommend reading this book in small bites! My book is already "dog-eared!"*
**– Tom Hayes, Ph.D., Dean, Williams College of Business, Xavier University**

# Praise for *The Fido Factor*

FIDO *will reenergize you with some doggone smart advice. Krissi and Dan Barr have captured the wisdom of dogs to get careers and businesses growing. Didn't we secretly always know that dogs were smarter than us? FIDO proves it!*
**– Lisa Hillenbrand, Marketing Consultant, Former Director Global Marketing, P&G**

*Who knew that you can boil down the secrets of being a great leader into our relationship with our canine friends? The Fido Factor is quick read, broken into bite-sized pieces, with wisdom for the aspiring or seasoned leader on every page. Well worth the read.*
**– Jim Schleckser, CEO of the Inc. CEO Project and author of Great CEOs Are Lazy**

*Perfect for any leader who wants to learn from the wisdom of dogs… or for any dog who wants to be a better leader. If you don't have a dog right now, you may soon be in the market for a new best friend…and future leader!*
**– Brian O. Underhill, Ph.D., CEO, CoachSource, author of Executive Coaching for Results: the Definitive Guide to Developing Organizational Leaders**

*Funny, insightful and loaded with practical ideas to help your entire team become more effective leaders.*
**– Steve Olberding, CEO, Phototype**

*To put it in dog terms,* The Fido Factor *is an A,B,C's about the many dynamics we all wrestle with in our lives. The correlation between a dog's world and our own makes this a fun and practical lesson in life…now sit!*
**– JB Buse, CEO, LOTH**

*A creative breakthrough, FIDO shatters the overworked leadership model with practical insight that's as entertaining as it is powerful. Even better, it will help you bark up the right tree.*
**– Steve Dilbone, Executive Director, Gradison Wealth Management**

*As a leadership instructor for two decades and a lifelong dog lover, I really, really enjoyed this book. Fun to read, excellent lessons and it definitely taught this old dog some new tricks.*
**– John Spence, author of Awesomely Simple and one of the top 100 Business Thought Leaders in America**

# Praise for *The Fido Factor*

# Table of Contents

*How many legs does a dog have if you call the tail a leg?*
*Four. Calling a tail a leg doesn't make it a leg.*
– Abraham Lincoln

# Preface

Calling a dog book a business leadership book doesn't make it one. It has to actually be one. Luckily, this really is a business leadership book. It just happens to have a dog theme.

Why dogs, you ask? Okay, fair question. After all, there aren't a lot of canine CEOs.

The main reason we're basing our book on dogs is because dogs have proven leadership genius. They instinctively know what personal qualities they need to develop in order to be their best. And they're naturals at exhibiting the traits needed to be leader of the pack.

It also helps that pretty much everyone can relate to dogs. And truth be told, most of us love dogs. This all adds up to a fresh take on leadership with insights that can have a profound impact on you as an individual and on your career as a leader.

To some, a business book with a dog theme may seem like a bit of a stretch. After all, they're just animals. What could humans — and especially business professionals — possibly learn from canines?

As it turns out, a lot. So unleash your preconceived notions and get ready for some tail-wagging good ideas about becoming the best leader you can be.

# The Fido Factor

There are more than two million different animal species on earth today, but humans have unquestionably formed their closest bond with one in particular: *Canis familiaris*. We call them dogs.

*Homo sapiens* and *Canis familiaris* have hit it off for time immemorial. They like us and we like them. When one talks, the other listens. We enjoy each other's company and respect each other's unique capabilities. We're on the same wavelength. Especially when we're on the same sofa.

There is tremendous diversity among both people and dogs. With all the different sizes, shapes and colors it's sometimes hard to believe we're all related. Yet, throughout that wide variety there are also common threads that link the most successful among us.

If you think about it, *leadership* is often the biggest differentiator when it comes to success. Without it, organizations can almost never succeed. With it, almost anything is possible.

Dogs have a natural genius for leadership. We arrived at this conclusion after many years of painstaking research, which included thousands of hours of ear scratching, throwing tennis balls and watching multiple seasons of dog shows on *Animal Planet*. More importantly, we studied canine behaviors and drilled down to discover the key lessons we can learn from them to help people become better leaders and get a leg up at work.

The leadership traits dogs embody can be boiled down to four themes: the Fido Factor.

## Faithful + Inspirational + Determined + Observant

*Faithful* leaders earn the trust of their team and their customers by doing the right things and living up to their word. *Inspirational* leaders move people to do the meaningful and the extraordinary. *Determined* leaders combine perseverance with a dose of fearlessness to keep moving toward goals. And *observant* leaders are committed to taking in as much information as possible in order to make the best decisions. These four dog-inspired traits are crucial to the success of every businessperson who wants to achieve his or her greatest potential.

To make this even easier to remember, here's a mnemonic device: the four Fido leadership factors — faithful, inspirational, determined and observant — spell out the name *Fido*. What are the odds?

This book digs deeply into each of the Fido Factors, combining individual development points with those for leading a team. True leadership, after all, starts with you. Your ability to command positions of authority and responsibility is based on your personal skills, qualities and traits.

To be an effective leader you must inspire others to listen to you, believe in you and follow you. That only happens when you lead by example.

When you've earned the right to lead others, that's when you'll face your most challenging test: leading your team of diverse individuals to success.

If you're like most business leaders, your team is essential to your success and survival. It's your customer service group, your field technicians, your salesforce, your accounts receivable department and your senior leadership team. Every day your squad straps on their gear and takes on the challenges of the marketplace.

Leadership is a team sport and the best leaders are always player-managers. It's time to put the best team on the field every day and inspire them to victory. It's time to lead like a dog.

# Faithful

Form a bond with a dog and you'll have a faithful friend forever. Someone you can depend on and who will defend you no matter what. When you are regarded as faithful it means you've earned trust. You can be relied upon.

Trust comes from being loyal to your teammates and customers, and doing what you say you're going to do when you say you'll do it. It's awfully hard to be an impactful leader if others don't think you're committed to the cause.

Unfaithful people may succeed in the short-term but they will never earn the trust and create the deep commitment of their team to be successful over the long haul. That matters because your career and reputation are the product of years of personal interactions and delivering results.

The difference between *management* and *leadership* is that effective managers get results while effective leaders get results through people…and the people feel good about it. This goes to the heart of team building. To get both results and loyal team members requires a personal connection based on your team's belief in you and what you stand for. You need to build trust to be influential and you need to be faithful to build trust.

Faithful leaders work in a way consistent with both their company and personal values. They don't spend sleepless nights worrying about what they said, how they acted or whether or not they did the right thing. That's because they make values-based choices that put the good of the team ahead of the personal interests of the leader.

## I'VE GOT YOUR TAIL

Dogs are pack animals. Put them in a group for a while and they form powerful bonds with both humans and other dogs. This strength-in-numbers approach has served them well for thousands of years.

While every pack has its own rules and culture, there are some universal truths. Most importantly, once you are a member of the pack, the pack will defend you against any threat.

*Chloe is a Longhaired Dachshund and one of the sweetest hounds anyone has ever met. She is an easy going pup who brings pure joy to the lives of the Oklahoma City high school teacher and golf professional she lives with.*

*That is until they all go for a walk. That's when Chloe transforms from mild-mannered pooch to the Ultimate Defender of the Pack. When Chloe sees someone walking toward them on the sidewalk, she starts to crouch down and prepares to take on the assailant. This is particularly bothersome when the "attacker" is an elderly neighbor out to pick up her morning newspaper at 5:50 AM.*

*In Chloe's mind she is doing what she needs to do. She's defending the pack. That's her job and she's going to make darn sure no one launches a surprise attack on anyone with a USA Today. Over the years her family has been able to soften Chloe's inclination to bark first and ask questions later, but there is no doubt in their minds that if they actually were attacked, they'd want Chloe there to defend them.*

It isn't easy to develop an "I've got your tail no matter the circumstances" attitude. Words are nice but they aren't enough. Just like dogs don't rely much on words, people don't either. What really matters are actions. Team leaders need to demonstrate their commitment to the group and their commitment to each individual member's success.

The best way to get commitments *from* your team is for you to make and keep commitments *to* your team. To get respect you have to give respect. Be the person who keeps appointments and rarely cancels or is late to meetings. When you cancel you're sending the message that whatever else you're doing matters more than your team member.

Doing what you say you're going to do when you say you're going to do it is the single most important aspect of trust. And when your true commitment to the team is repeated over and over, it becomes part of your leadership presence.

Surround yourself with people whose word is their bond and you'll have a high trust work environment. That makes everything easier. In addition, productivity, morale and engagement all increase.

Show the pack by your actions that what's best for the team supersedes what's best for you. Regularly demonstrate you will do whatever is necessary to make the success of the entire organization your top priority. It all starts with each member of the team knowing you've got their tail.

- How do you show that you put the team's needs ahead of your own?
- How do you regularly demonstrate that you will do whatever is necessary to defend your pack?

## WEAR IT ON YOUR COLLAR

Dogs let us know how much they care for us. They don't hide their feelings. If you are feeling low, somehow they sense it, come over, lie in your lap and lick you until you feel better.

*Shakespeare, a tri-colored Foxhound, seems to have a sixth sense. He knows things most dogs aren't aware of. This may be related to the fact that he understands English. That having been said, he really needs to work on his ability to enunciate clearly.*

*Anyway, he can sense when his family members are upset. It's likely a combination of his ability to sense emotions — from tone of voice and body language — plus his uncanny ability to comprehend lines from* The Merchant of Venice, *like "O, what a goodly outside falsehood hath!"*

*When Shakespeare senses someone's mad, he generally steers clear for a few minutes. He is, after all, a very smart dog. There's no sense in getting in the middle of someone else's mess. But then when things calm down, he comes over and gives the formerly miffed person that "I know you're upset, so why don't you pet me and I'll lick you and everyone will feel better" look.*

*Lo! Forsooth, it works every time.*

Do the same with your colleagues. Not the licking, just the caring. It can be as simple as asking "How are you doing?" But the key is doing it with sincerity. The tone of your voice and your body language will convey more than the words themselves. If you want people to believe you care about them, you have to actually care.

You may wonder if, as the lead dog, you should show any signs of emotions or vulnerability. Woof yes! It makes you more authentic. And authentic leaders are seen as more competent leaders.

It's important to be curious about each member of the pack. If you see unusual behaviors, ask them what's going on and how you can help. Then listen intently to what's being said and not said. When you wear it on your collar by showing you care you can't help but build a stronger team.

- How can you demonstrate every day that you genuinely care about others?
- How can you learn what your team really cares about?

## MUSH

Business is a team sport. Someone creates, another sells, and yet another delivers. There's a billing department, a collections group and the people in charge of accounting and finance. And don't forget about human resources, marketing, logistics, operations, legal, product development and all the other critical elements that make most successful companies excel at what they do.

And when everyone is working together and communicating effectively — two vital functions of senior management — remarkable things can happen.

*The Iditarod is the world's most famous annual dog sled race. The eleven hundred-mile journey across the wilderness of Alaska is an epic test of strength, endurance and determination.*

*Each team is led by a musher. That's the human who yells "mush" to get the dogs moving. I guess "sled driver" and "sled team leader" were already trademarked. Or maybe dogs really do respond better to the 5:00 AM call of "mush!" than "Okay dogs, we've got one hundred miles to run today, so let's get going!"*

*Of critical importance, each team consists of sixteen dogs whose job it is to pull the sled from Anchorage to Nome. Since most people haven't made that trek, it's like going from Boston to Atlanta. In the snow.*

*Not all dogs are well suited for these conditions. It's hard to imagine a team of Toy Poodles and Chihuahuas getting out of the parking lot in Anchorage. Fortunately, Siberian Huskies are very well suited to this line of work.*

The key to winning at the Iditarod and in business is teamwork. So why are some teams more successful than others? It starts at the top. Good leaders assemble the right teams for the job. And then they manage them by setting realistic goals, coaching each person and supporting the team with resources. After all, if you want to win the Iditarod you'd better have a good sled and some terrific, well-trained dogs.

Teams by their very nature bring more resources, ideas and energy to a challenge. They can accomplish far more than an individual going it alone. Teams, when structured and managed properly, can synthesize the best ideas into a breakthrough new product or service.

As the leader, you need to bring together a team that has the skills and mindsets necessary to complete the project at hand. Typically a good mix includes people with expertise in technical, sales and marketing, operational and financial disciplines. For big projects, look for representatives with diverse backgrounds to open up thinking even further.

There are many different ways to manage a team, and choosing the right style often depends on the specifics. In general, to reach your destination make sure the following are in place:
- Clear and measurable goals
- Timetables for accomplishing milestones
- Well-defined roles and responsibilities
- Budgets and resources
- Reporting timeframe and format

Once everyone is on board, your job as the leader is to motivate, encourage, arbitrate, discipline and generally keep things on course. If you abdicate your role as musher, teamwork will almost always degenerate into chaos. That's usually when you realize you're in Juneau, not Nome.

- What specific things do you do to foster teamwork in your workplace?
- What do you need to add to facilitate teamwork (e.g. milestones, timetables, defined roles, budgets, reporting formats, face-to-face meetings)?

*Money can buy you a fine dog,*
*but only love can make him wag his tail.*
– Kinky Friedman

## THE BONDS THAT BIND

One of the most endearing parts of the human-canine connection is the way we build relationships. With people and their pets, the relationship often starts with a puppy. We love it, play with it, groom it, feed it and care for it. Along the way, a special bond is built. It is a covenant of trust and mutual self-defense.

*When Jeff, a VP of Sales with a software company, went on a three day business trip with his new regional sales manager, it was an important bonding experience. He got to see his manager interact with customers, helped close a new deal and learned why Kansas City is famous for its barbeque.*

*A similar thing happened when Jeff took his puppy to Cape Cod for the first time. Baxter, a twenty-five pound rescue, took to the ocean like he had been born with fins. Here was this amazing place, filled with new sights, sounds, smells and sensations. Baxter chased the gulls, dodged the waves and harassed the crabs. Then did it over and over again.*

*Every early morning walk on the beach was an adventure for both Jeff and Baxter. More than that, it brought them closer together.*

To lead others at work you need to build relationships. Everyone is looking for shortcuts, but there aren't many. Having friends or experiences in common helps, but nothing beats the ordinary and extraordinary things that are discovered together. It takes time to develop a deep relationship and you have to want it. If you are willing to put in the effort, you'll have teammates at work who will do anything for you. And vice versa.

Dogs have their own unique way of getting to know newcomers. They start by checking each other out. This often involves a lot of sniffing, sometimes in embarrassing places. Following that they establish dominance. This can take the form of barking and aggressive posturing. Then it's time to get on with the day and chase the Doberman with the tennis ball.

Just like dogs, people crave friendships and positive interactions. So it makes sense that the better our relationships, the happier and more productive we are going to be at work.

You want to know what makes the other person tick. Find out what they enjoy doing in their spare time, learn about their family and uncover what you have in common. It always helps when you look someone in the eye and really listen to what they say.

The easiest way to get to know people is to work shoulder to shoulder and have worthwhile conversations. Here are some tips:
- Show genuine appreciation for their contributions
- Be positive and smile
- Don't gossip
- Find common interests
- Be empathetic
- Be sincere
- Ask open-ended questions to draw out a conversation
- Don't multitask

Even with the most standoffish people, don't give up. It only takes one person to warm up a cold relationship, so be that person. Building meaningful relationships is critical to the long-term success of your team. If you put your paws into it, you're bound to succeed.

- How well do you really know the people with whom you regularly work?
- How can you put in the time and effort to build strong bonds with co-workers?

## ATTENTION SEEKERS

One of the things most dog people do, often without even thinking about it, is interact with their pets on a frequent basis. This high-frequency attention, even if it is just for a brief moment, keeps us connected. And while it's important for older dogs, it's especially critical to the bonding process for puppies.

*We talk to our dogs. A lot. And they're never shy about talking back to us. For example, when we see them after a day at work we often say "How was your day? Did you have fun?" Their answer is always the same: "Yes we had a fantastic day, we're happy to see you, let's pour some fresh water in the dish and celebrate!"*

*When we walk around our house, if we pass a dog lounging on a sofa, we give them a quick pet on the head. If we aren't rushing out the door we'll stop to deliver a ten-second belly rub or toss a toy down the front hallway. Little things throughout the day to acknowledge that they are there with us and we care about them.*

The same idea applies to interactions with your co-workers. A few positive words every chance you get goes a long way toward building bonds, establishing loyalty and creating an environment of mutual trust.

Be sure to spend regular one-on-one time with your closest team members to give them the attention they need and deserve. Schedule these sessions as reoccurring meetings to make them predictable. And try not to cancel when something "more urgent" comes up. The agenda is easy:

- How are you? What's new?
- How are your people doing?
- What is the most important thing we should be talking about today?
- What are your priorities?
- Here's what you did well.
- Here's what you can add to what you are doing.
- What did you accomplish since the last time we met?
- What do you plan to accomplish between now and the next time we meet?
- What do you need from me? How can I support you?
- Here are my priorities so you'll know what I'm working on.

People, like dogs, crave attention. It's important to be fully present in those one-on-ones. That means resisting the urge to check your phone every time it buzzes. Go into the meeting thinking this is a chance to further build the relationship and evaluate progress on projects. Even more than attention, people love recognition for a job well done, so be sure to express gratitude and celebrate wins.

The opposite of attention is silence, invisibility and a sense that what your team members are doing doesn't matter. If that ever sets in, you will have a team engagement and morale crisis brewing. Luckily, you can avoid this by just giving your group lots of attention.

- In what ways do you give your co-workers enough personal attention so they know how important they are?
- How productive and consistent are your one-on-one meetings?

## KISS

The dictionary is full of words that describe people. Many of those words zero in on mankind's multitude of negative traits and behaviors. Only one word in the English language is "perfect," and that doesn't get used a lot.

Sure, we try. At work we strive for that annual review where we exceeded our goals and received "exceptional" ratings on all of our personal characteristic measurements.

But, alas, the perfect review is very rare. We are flawed. So are our co-workers. It's easy to see the shortcomings in others and a little harder to see them in ourselves.

One of the things we love about dogs is how non-judgmental they are. They don't care if we gain ten pounds or dress up like Darth Vader at Comic-Con. They love us for who we really are.

*Stanley is a black and white Boxer with a distinguishing splotch that covers his right eye. It was this unique coloration that attracted Frank, a tax attorney and avowed KISS fan, when he first saw the puppy.*

*As any KISS fan knows, Paul Stanley is the band's lead singer. On stage he's the one with the star painted around his eye. Not to be confused with the guy with the long tongue, the one with the spaceman motif or the one who looks like a cat. We are not making this stuff up.*

*Anyway, every year Frank throws a big party where all his friends dress up as their favorite KISS persona, listen to songs like* Rock 'n Roll All Nite *and* Love Gun *at high volume and drink KISS Shout It Out Chardonnay and KISS Zin Fire Zinfandel.*

*Stanley, of course, loves a good party. And every year when the last absurdly festooned friend has left and* Detroit Rock City *is back in its album sleeve, Stanley curls up next to Frank on the couch. Who cares if his cat makeup is smearing?*

At work, we need to make decisions, not judgments. Should we go with the new edits on the ad campaign or do another rewrite? Apply another coat of white paint to the wall or is the old turquoise color completely covered? Make an offer to a new hire or keep searching for a better candidate?

There's a difference between behaviors and judgments. Behaviors can be seen, while judgments are inferred. Judgments often leave a lot of room for misinterpretation, can make people defensive and harm our ability to work as a team.

Words matter and some words can hurt. "That's bad," "You're an idiot," and "I hate that" are ideal phrases to use when you want to alienate those around you and lousy words to use when you are trying to build teamwork. When communicating with co-workers eliminate all judgment words and use only words that are about tangible behaviors.

Words can have different meanings and interpretations, which is why communication can break down. What is intended to be a factual statement may be received by the other person as a mean-spirited judgment. To improve your clarity, try saying what you normally say then add "…and by that I mean…" Your personal leadership quotient will increase with clearer communications.

It's a big world out there, with many different cultures, religions, lifestyles and tastes in music. Managing a diverse workforce can get complicated. Good leaders embrace the challenge and follow the KISS principle. They put their non-judgmental mindset on display every day. And never forget, one person's *I Was Made For Lovin' You* is another's reason to *Shout It Out Loud* to the human resources department.

- Are you in the habit of expressing snap judgments, and if so, how can you curtail that?
- What words should you eliminate from your work vocabulary?

## LOYALTY IN THE AGE OF FREE AGENTS

Go for a walk with your dogs and you're likely to see one of their strong suits: loyalty. They will defend you from the oncoming kid on a bike, the baby stroller approaching from behind and the Pug barking in the neighbor's window. And while we don't always do what our dogs want, they never turn on us.

*Bella can be a little hard to figure out sometimes. As a rescue, no one's really sure what type of dog she is, but her long hair, alert eyes and big paws point toward her having some retriever in her. Walk in the room and she displays her instinctive skittishness. But once you pet her, she smiles and wants more. She has to be reminded ten times a day that everything is fine, unless she chewed up the mail.*

*Once she is in her safe place, Bella lets her loyalty flag fly high. She will do anything for her family members. If they drop food on the floor, she is more than happy to clean it up. If there are squirrels in the back yard, she is honored to protect the pack by chasing them into the woods. And if someone calls her, she comes. Especially when they have a Pup-peroni in hand.*

*Ain't loyalty grand?*

Loyalty at work is more difficult to achieve. That's because the dynamic is different. Your dog isn't going to dump you for another home, but your employees can leave any time they want. True loyalty is built when you demonstrate your commitment to the other person's success.

There are many ways to show loyalty. Promoting from within, providing career and professional development, even investing in new furniture and equipment: all demonstrate the desire to strengthen the entire organization.

The only way to build *dog* loyalty is to demonstrate your total commitment to your pack, and that takes work and sacrifice. When times are tough, loyalty is tested. Companies may be able to avoid letting go of associates by temporarily reducing executive compensation, eliminating unnecessary travel and delaying capital investments. The key during belt tightening is to find a way to consistently send the message that the team is loyal to each individual member.

Loyalty is different from engagement. *Engagement* is when associates feel connected to their work, company, purpose and vision. *Loyalty* is when you and your team members run through fences for each other and won't jump ship when another company offers a modest increase in pay.

When you have loyal partners it has a powerful impact on your customers, too. They see a supplier with happier and more passionate team members. The upshot of that is they're less likely to switch to a competitor just because they are a little cheaper or you dropped the ball on one project.

To build loyalty, develop your company's vision or purpose statement and then deliver on that promise. Invest in team development, delegate more and involve others in key decisions. In addition to loyalty you'll reap the benefits of increased productivity and revenue growth.

Ralph Waldo Emerson said "What you do speaks so loud that I cannot hear what you say." When it comes to loyalty, actions really do speak louder than words.

- What messages do you need to send others to build long-term loyalty?
- What can you learn about loyalty from analyzing employee and customer turnover rates?

## THE RATTLESNAKE TEST

We don't test our dog's courage every day. We don't have to. We know it will be there should we ever need it.

*Taffy is a Cocker Spaniel who lives in San Diego. She's a snuggler. Her magnetic smile and wavy brown hair make her irresistible to everyone who meets her.*

*One weekend she was hiking with her people in Torrey Pines State Park, the glorious spot of land overlooking the Pacific Ocean just north of town. When there was no one else around, Taffy would be let off her leash, and she loved to run ahead to survey the situation.*

*One such time she went around a bend and froze. There was a rattlesnake sunning itself on the path. Taffy began to bark, warning her companions of the danger ahead.*

*Apparently the snake didn't like having its nap interrupted, and began to hiss. It also started rattling its tail. Upon seeing a rattlesnake menacing their beloved Taffy — the sweetest little dog ever, they always said — the humans freaked out.*

*Taffy didn't back down. She barked and snarled and menaced right back. There was no way she'd let that snake attack her people.*

*And it didn't. Eventually the snake decided it wasn't worth taking on opponents larger than it could swallow, so it slithered off into the brush. Taffy found her human friends especially affectionate and generous with table scraps that night.*

Your co-workers don't regularly come face-to-face with rattlesnakes in the normal course of business. But courage in the face of adversity is an underappreciated virtue. Threats of all types cross our paths. Some people choose to avoid a course that could possibly pose a risk. Others turn and run when frightened. And yet others stand their ground, defend their turf and protect their teammates.

You exhibit courage any time you do what's right, especially if no one is watching. It takes guts to say the new product won't be ready by the launch date. It takes nerve to politely stand up to a customer who is berating your team after they delivered exactly what was asked. It takes bravery to speak up when you know the numbers aren't right.

Leaders have the intestinal fortitude to confront problems. They have difficult conversations to address important matters, not avoid them. They know they have to be frank but diplomatic. When necessary they take unpopular stands and say no when everyone else is saying yes.

It takes courage to show vulnerability. That's why asking for help can be a sign of strength.

In the long run, when you are courageous, you are acting in the best interest of the company and everyone who works with you.

- When have you shown the courage to stand up against what is wrong or dangerous?
- What is a difficult situation you are facing now where you need to take an unpopular position?

## FOR THE GOOD OF THE PACK

Dogs have a generosity streak a mile wide. That is unless there's a pound cake on the floor and two dogs going after it. In that case, it's every dog for itself, and get ready to hide when the family comes home.

*When interacting with people, dogs exhibit their unselfishness. They will gladly share a bowl of nachos with their favorite person (easy on the jalapenos, hombre). At bedtime they are happy to let the human pick a spot on the bed, as they can curl up anywhere. And if the person on the other end of the leash doesn't like rain, it's okay to cut short a walk. To a dog it's all about what's good for the pack.*

At work we have to find the right balance between being unselfish and not being a pushover. If you played a major role in landing a big new account, don't be afraid to take some credit. But if landing a new customer was a team effort, then share the glory. And maybe the commission, too.

In order to be less selfish we need to be generous with our time. When a co-worker or a customer needs help, try offering assistance before they ask. Collaborate and share information even when it might not be in your personal best interest. Be modest and focus on how you can assist others. After all, everyone loves the humble hero.

- How can you share the spotlight more with others in your team?
- How can you help someone else accomplish their goals?

## RULES RULE

Compliance is important for everyone. Just like some people rebel at conformity, so do dogs. In the canine world compliance can mean everything from having current dog tags to not taking a poop on the carpet. Dogs need to be taught the rules required for a happy assimilation into what is a very human-dominated world.

At work, we need to learn the rules, too. And follow them. Turn in your expense reports promptly, properly fill out your time sheets and report to work at the designated time.

*When she was a puppy, Lucy, a two-toned Airedale, liked to chew. After experimenting early on with fingers and socks, Lucy's chomp of choice eventually turned to furniture and floor coverings. She seemed to have a particular affinity for nice stuff, like Persian rugs, the legs of Chippendale chairs and anything that looked like it belonged on Antiques Roadshow.*

*Her family members were not pleased with this behavior so they gave her a chew-toy. Lucy ignored it. Over numerous subsequent trips to the pet store her family bought nearly every dog toy ever made. Some squeaked, some bounced, and some were meat flavored. All were sniffed, surveyed and quickly ignored.*

*By the time Lucy's family had purchased their third rug for the entry hallway — each one costing half as much as the last — she began to get out of her chewing phase. Her puppy teeth had been replaced by adult ones and her desire to gnaw on things was waning. And that's a good thing, because her family was almost ready to put an old towel inside the front door.*

Compliance is difficult for some people, like putting a steak in front of a hungry dog and telling it to wait to eat. At work, adherence to the rules matters because people follow the leader's example. When no one follows the rules, bedlam ensues.

Every business has its own norms. Maybe executives wear a suit and tie except on casual

Fridays when they lose the tie. If so, forget the tie on Fridays. Compliance helps make things more predictable, and as companies get bigger and more complex, that's not all bad.

Compliance fosters unity and order while providing the structures that support reliability and quality. Adhering to traditions, rules and procedures can mitigate business and reputational risks while building trust.

It helps to understand the reasons why compliance is important. If you're new to an industry, it may feel onerous to jump through a few extra hoops, but perhaps it's essential to stay within the law. Maybe your company doesn't allow eating lunch at your desk. If so, it would be good to know that's because customers regularly tour the headquarters.

Annually review all the rules to determine if they still make sense. If a rule is outdated, get rid of it. People will thank you. And if you need to add some systems and structures, do that too. You're striving for compliance with flexibility.

- What areas of non-compliance do you need to work on?
- What rules or procedures should you eliminate?

## FETCH

Few games are more appealing to dogs than fetch. Whether it's a tennis ball, a stick or a newspaper, dogs love it. They get to run, they get to play, and if you let them keep score, they always win.

Fetch in the human world is defined as to go out, get something and bring it back. Sounds a lot like sales if you think about it.

Generating revenue is a vital element for any company. While most organizations have salespeople, the skills required to bring in purchase orders apply far beyond your sales and marketing department.

Every true leader is in sales. It doesn't matter if your job description has nothing to do with making the cash register ring, you are selling every day. You sell your ideas, your ability to excel at a job and, most importantly, yourself as a trusted member of the team.

*Cooper is a Havanese and a master at wooing people. When there's a party at his house he has the ability to shift effortlessly from mild-mannered chaser of squirrels into salesdog extraordinaire.*

*He always makes a point of greeting each guest personally when they arrive. That way he feels like the living room isn't full of strangers, only a few people who smell strange.*

*Cooper immediately sets out to make new friends. He meets each person and tries to connect. One person pats him on the head. Another tosses him a squeaky toy and gets a game going. Still another sneaks him a piece of cheese off the tray.*

*As the night goes on, Cooper goes back to each guest, trying to assess what else can the two of them do, and, most importantly, how he is going to coax that last piece of meat off their plate. Cooper is known for his excellent closing techniques.*

People are influenced by and purchase from people they know, like and trust. Building these relationships takes effort: meeting people repeatedly, being there when they need you, helping them accomplish their goals and finding what unique interests they have. And it always pays off.

Work is a series of interactions with other people, departments, companies and cultures. If you can improve your ability to influence and persuade others on your ideas you'll achieve more success.

- How can you become more effective at persuading others?
- How do you earn the trust of others?

## RECHARGE THE BATTERIES

On one level, a dog's life is simple. They eat when hungry, drink when thirsty, play whenever possible and sleep when tired. The next day they do it all over again. Not a bad gig if you can get it.

People do that, too. When we're on vacation, that is. Unfortunately, ninety-five percent of the time we're not.

Work-life balance is important. Work is a key component of life, but if it causes major family disruptions or brings about health problems, something has to change.

*Gloria is a Basset Hound who lives with a cat and two very nice people.*

*Some days she joins the people on a car trip that goes to "doggy day care," which is people-speak for "dog party." There she runs around with her friends, sniffing and barking and generally having an enjoyable time doing dog things.*

*When she's tired, she goes off and finds a soft blanket to take a nap. When rested, she gets back in the game. The cat has no idea how much fun he is missing.*

It isn't easy juggling all the things in our lives. Work, children, significant other, exercise, cooking, shopping, cleaning, and sleeping: everything takes time. It's easy to get out of balance.

That's when you need to stop and prioritize. You have to be physically well or you won't be your best in any aspect of your life. This means finding the time to eat healthy food, workout and get enough sleep.

There are times when work seems to take over our lives. And some of that is okay, like when you are maxed out the month before a big project is due. Just make sure a frenzied pace isn't your new normal. You need some exhale time, too. The *all on or all off* approach to work gives most people the respite they need. The key is to find the mix of work-life integration that works for you.

Some ideas to give you the space to recharge include not overcommitting to too many things and spending at least thirty minutes daily doing something you love (that's only 2% of a day). You can also set boundaries on what you will or won't do and say "no" to draining activities.

Whether you're the CEO or a temp in a factory, you need some down time. For you that might mean going fishing with your kids, camping with your spouse or going for a run with your dog. Afterwards you'll come back to work with more energy, enthusiasm and a new burst of creativity. That's good for business and it's good for your health. Work hard, play hard and chill.

- What do you need to change in your routine to give you more "you" time?
- What things should you do to recharge yourself every day?

## THE VET WILL SEE YOU NOW

Veterinarians are doctors, and we take our dogs to see them to make sure they stay healthy. Vets do both preventative and curative medicine. Regular checkups, distemper shots and monthly flea and tick medicine all make for a happy, healthy dog.

Humans need to do the same. Get regular check-ups, take your meds, see the dentist every six months…all good advice. If you don't it will likely catch up with you. And that will have a negative impact on your work.

*When you think about it, being a veterinarian is a pretty tough job. Your patients range from parakeets to horses and none of them can tell you where it hurts.*

*Most dogs don't like going to the vet. Maybe it's because of how they get their temperature taken.*

*Quincy, a black Lab, wasn't acting like his normal self. He was walking funny and seemed hesitant to go upstairs at his family's home in Tuscaloosa, so they went to see their local vet. His family knew Labs were prone to hip dysplasia and they were concerned he may have chronic pain and problems.*

*Upon arriving at the vet's office, Quincy's normally positive attitude changed. He hated seeing the vet and tried mightily to persuade his family to get back in the car and go somewhere else. Anywhere else.*

*In the course of Dr. Kim's examination she made a surprising discovery: a small burr was wedged in between Quincy's hind paws. A quick pluck with a pair of tweezers and their old pal was as good as new.*

There may be things you don't enjoy doing, either at the doctor's office or at work. But you need to do them for your health and for the health of your company.

You can prevent some health problems by developing good wellness habits. Other things happen because of genetics or accidents and are often unavoidable. Regardless, developing a proactive approach to your own health will serve you well and keep you leading at peak performance.

Set a good example by taking time to take care of yourself. Encourage those around you to get flu shots, physicals and regular mammograms or colonoscopies. Send people home who are sick so they can get well…and not pass on whatever they have to the rest of the organization.

- How are you prioritizing your own health and the health of those you care about?
- What regular checkups do you need to schedule?

## PURPOSE

Your dog has a purpose in your life. Generally speaking it is to provide you with a loving companion, to feel your reciprocated love and to make sure you don't sleep too late on the weekends.

You have a purpose in your dog's life. You are there to care for it, to love it and to prevent it from getting into the clothes hamper and chewing up your favorite socks.

*Dogs seem to have a sixth sense, a mysterious way of knowing things they otherwise wouldn't know. Glen, a manager at a manufacturing company, experienced this a few years ago while recovering after a minor surgery.*

*He was recuperating at his home in Coral Gables by lying on the sofa and watching Australian rules football on television. Under normal circumstances Zoe, his Bichon Frise, would bring one of her toys and try to get a game of fetch going.*

*But Zoe seemed to sense something was different. Maybe it was the blanket Glen had covered himself with or the smell of the bandages. Regardless, Zoe just snuggled up and let the healing process continue. It was as if she knew her job was to just be there. Even if that meant doing nothing for a change.*

At work, each of us has a purpose, too. If you are in sales, for example, your basic reason for being at the company is to sell. So resolve to be the best at it.

You should have a higher purpose, too. Something that gives meaning and drives you and your entire organization.

A company's purpose encapsulates what you really do for your customers. More specifically, it speaks to how everyone in your organization positively impacts the lives of the people you serve. It needs to be something you are proud of and will stand the test of time.

A recruiting services company's purpose may be "to help others find their destiny." A hospital's purpose could be "to save lives in our community."

Your company's purpose should underscore why your organization exists and provide significance and meaning to what you do. On a personal level it should resonate with your values and reinforce why you are part of the team. Once you are crystal clear on what your company's purpose is, embrace it and pursue it with everything you have.

- What is your company's purpose?
- How do you communicate your purpose to your customers, prospects, recruits and associates?

## TO THE END

They say the average dog lives 12 years. That, of course, is an incorrect statement because there are no average dogs. Especially not the ones you live with.

They also say the end of a dog's life is one of the most difficult periods that can be experienced. Sadly, this is absolutely true. The slow decline of a beloved pet through old age forces us to rethink diets, play time and mobility. Their final passing gives us the unwanted opportunity to grieve.

Nothing is guaranteed in life, with the possible exception of the total love and devotion of your dog. After losing a faithful friend, often the best way to get past the hurt is to bring a new puppy into the home.

*Max, a Westie Terrier, was getting old. He lumbered slowly around the house, wouldn't hop onto the sofa and stopped bounding up the stairs.*

*His family tried everything: senior dog food, extra visits to the vet, acupuncture and even little steps up to the bed. They seemed to help. But eventually Max took a turn for the worse.*

*He had been an essential part of his family's life for what seemed like forever. It hurt like hell to let go.*

New hire paperwork does not include a clause that says "hired for life." And yet we want our best associates to be a part of the team for as long as possible.

In the real world, things happen. People get hurt and sick. And way more often than not they make a full recovery and rejoin the team. Real leaders keep a seat warm for their co-workers who need the time to recuperate.

Caring leaders find a way to help their people who are not coming back, too. They do it because it is compassionate and good and right. It also sends a message to everyone else in the workplace: we are family.

- How do you show support for associates who are battling illness?
- What are some ways you could demonstrate to your team that they really are like family to you?

# Faithful

**Faithful leaders are:**
- Loyal
- Trustworthy
- Caring

**Faithful leaders succeed because they:**
- Do the right thing, even when no one's watching.
- Defend their pack no matter what.
- Do what they say they're going to do when they say they're going to do it.
- Put the needs of customers and team members ahead of their own.
- Invest time in building and growing relationships.
- Clearly define measurable expectations to facilitate teamwork.
- Balance flexibility with compliance.
- Develop and communicate a higher purpose for the work being done.
- Value downtime to recharge.

**Faithful leaders are respected because they:**
- Have the courage to confront problems and speak the truth.
- Know it's a sign of strength to ask for help.
- Are modest and share the spotlight.
- Lead by example.
- Genuinely care about others.
- Earn trust and are not judgmental.
- Put a priority on their own health and the wellbeing of others.
- Send the message that the pack is family.
- Show loyalty to others in a multitude of ways.

*If there are no dogs in Heaven, then when I die
I want to go where they went.*
– Will Rogers

## FIDO FACTOR
# Inspirational

Dogs are naturally inspirational. They make us feel good, lift our spirits and energize us to our very core. Selfless, motivational and with a tail that always speaks the truth, dogs make us believe anything is possible. To maximize your leadership role you have to inspire greatness in others by getting them to believe they can do what they thought was impossible.

Inspiration moves people to do the extraordinary. As a leader you need to have and articulate a compelling vision that matters to your team and your customers. Inspirational leaders can see where they want to be in the future. They are enthusiastic and optimistic about realizing the vision and find a way to ignite the same passion in others. Inspirational leaders change the question from "What's in it for me?" to "What's in it for us!"

Inspirational leaders craft the specific steps that will get the organization across the finish line. They include team members in the creation of goals and action plans in order to build buy-in and ownership.

Inspirational leaders realize people need an environment where they can take smart chances in order to innovate, as mistakes bring success closer. They foster collaboration and idea sharing while building a culture that embraces diverse thinking and learning. Inspirational leaders know they have to strike the right balance between short-term interests and the path toward achieving the long-term vision.

Inspiration is unique to each person. What pumps you up may not work for someone else. That's why it's such a challenge to inspire people to follow you. And yet inspirational leaders find a way to develop engaged and happy co-workers who know their individual contributions matter.

## GREET 'EM LIKE YOU MEAN IT

When you come home, your dog is always there to say hello. Not just a "Hey, how was your day?" but a jump in the air, bark like crazy and twirl around "I am deliriously happy to see you!" kind of greeting.

*If one of us tells our dogs someone is coming home, they totally get it. They run to the front door to wait, giddy with anticipation. It's like telling a child that Santa is about to come down the chimney with a sack full of Christmas presents.*

*Our dogs will wait at the door for hours. Clearly they need to work on their grasp of timing, but they really don't mind. What they want is to be there and jump for joy when we walk through the threshold. Ah, home sweet home.*

Do the same at work! Okay, you may not want to twirl around, but you get the idea.

When co-workers come back to the office after a tough meeting with a client, show them you are genuinely happy to see them.

Happiness, fun and optimism are choices. And when you show you are happy, it's as contagious as fleas, in a good way. Everyone can feel the joy and lower stress levels.

At the end of the day, before you go to sleep, ask yourself "What made me happy today?" It will reinforce the good things that are happening versus obsessing over what can go wrong.

Ideas to improve happiness can be as simple as asking your team members to rate their happiness on a scale of one to five. After they give you their answer, then ask, "What made you give it that rating?" For anything less than a four, ask them for two specific ideas on actions that could be done to improve their happiness quotient. And then implement some of those ideas. You'll discover many new things about your company, your leadership style and your team.

Better yet, your company will probably realize improved retention and profits as by-products. There's a reason why some successful companies are known for their happiness culture. You and your team spend an enormous amount of time at work. It should be a place where you and others are happy.

Employees do more when they feel appreciated and connected to the organization on a deeper level than just doing their job and collecting a paycheck. When they are aligned with the company's objectives they go the extra mile with customers and they work more effectively as a team. They are engaged.

The problem is that real engagement is hard to pull off. Co-workers have to believe you are truly committed to the pack and that you care about them personally. Just like a dog can tell when someone is untrustworthy, your associates will sniff you out if you are inauthentic.

As the lead dog, you set the tone. That can be a welcoming, positive culture or a "leave me alone and get back to work" environment.

While every leader wants their team to be more engaged, the question of how to do that is much simpler to answer when you put it in dog terms. A dog only becomes fully engaged with its pack based on consistent and positive interaction. So every day, be sure to press the flesh, chew the fat and throw the tennis ball. Engagement will follow.

It's easy to choose to be happy. Smile more. Don't use negative self-talk or language. Put things in perspective and stop overreacting to minor irritations. Help other people with their problems. Be nice and polite. Build people up and wag your tail when something goes right. It's those little things that matter most and have the biggest impact.

- How do you show genuine happiness to your team?
- In what ways do you choose to be happy on a daily basis?

## ATTITUDE IS EVERYTHING

Dogs can't help it: they're just naturally enthusiastic and optimistic. Everything they put their paws into is done with passion and an unbridled positive spirit.

*Charlie is a brown Labradoodle in Austin. His favorite toy is nicknamed "Jack." It's a blue plastic object that bounces in crazy ways and resembles the iconic six-pronged children's toy.*

*To say Charlie is obsessed with Jack is an understatement. It's almost all he thinks about. His favorite game is fetch. Played, of course, with his Jack. Charlie will play with it until he's exhausted, so it's up to his family to know when to stop. He has two speeds: on and totally Jacked-up.*

Our thoughts can create the future. John Miller of Velocity fame gave us this formula:

## Events + Choices = Results

Events happen. When they're combined with the choices you make — how you think and act — that's what determines the result. You control one hundred percent of what you think and how you act. Choice is a gift, so choose to have the right attitude.

People will be attracted to you and you'll be more approachable when you have a positive attitude. When you think about what you want to accomplish, you are in control of your future. When you think about what you don't want, you are more likely to be frustrated and feel like a victim of circumstance.

If you have a negative person in your group, reframe their negative "don't want" comments into future-focused "do want" comments. For example, if someone says "I don't want to stay inside my crate all day" you can pivot that to "Sounds like you want to go outside and run today." Try to learn what the root cause of the negativity is. Ask the person how you can help change that mindset and talk about how their behaviors are affecting the team.

Begin each day with encouraging thoughts about what you want to accomplish. See yourself doing the activities that will get you there. Don't let any negative attitudes or habits get in your way. Have both a "can do" and "will do" mindset. Even if you're facing the tallest fence you've ever had to leap over (or dig under), ask yourself how this can be the best problem you've ever had because now you have the opportunity to use your innovation skills.

When you have a positive attitude it sets an example to help others achieve more than they thought was possible. Optimists imagine success and view adversity as temporary. A winning outlook boosts productivity, improves morale and grows profits. And frankly it just feels good to wag your tail.

Ever see a dog half-tail it? Nope. Dogs go after activities with full-throttled enthusiasm. They give maximum effort whether it's going for a walk or looking for a thrown ball. Dogs go all out until they are really tired, and only then do they take a break.

We need to do the same at work. Granted, entering data onto a spreadsheet doesn't evoke the same natural enthusiasm as playing fetch in the park, but find a way to channel your inner dog.

Attitude is infectious, so start with yours. Commit yourself to approaching everything you do with gusto. When the rest of your team sees you aren't just going through the motions they'll want to join in on the fun.

Workers at every level want to contribute to something big and meaningful. The carpenter who did framing on a few floors of a one hundred-story building takes pride in the finished skyscraper. For a business to achieve its goals you'll need people to see how their individual contributions and positive attitude keeps customers and makes phenomenal things happen.

Before you approach your next activity, think about what level of effort is needed to do your best. Your energy and attitude directly impact the energy and attitude of those around you.

Enthusiasm, like happiness, is contagious. And a lot less dangerous than kennel cough. Spread some.

- How do you choose to approach things: from a positive "will do" mindset or an obstacle "that won't work" mindset?
- What steps do you need to take to exude a more positive attitude for yourself and within your team?

## TALE OF THE TAIL

One of the things we love most about a dog is its tail. It's a crystal clear barometer of how the pooch is feeling. Happy and it wags like crazy. Guilty and it curls under out of shame.

People are much harder to read. Often we keep our cards close to the vest, not wanting to show the world how we truly feel. And while there are times when that makes sense, to build a great performance team you need to show how you feel. Over half of our communications comes from our body language, so when you withhold emotion, the message you're conveying is probably not the one you intended.

When dogs do something wrong they admit it. Dogs can't tell a lie. You know if they made a mess in the bedroom just from looking at them. They won't look you in the eye, they don't wag their tail. They can't hide it. And when they are happy they really show it!

*Churchill is a Bulldog with a white and brown coat and a stiff upper lip.*

*When one of his human family members goes out of town, Churchill's high-powered mind goes into overdrive. He gets depressed, sometimes to the point of being downright mad. When this happens, he likes to go into the bedroom of the person who left and "express his anger." This expression is typically in the form of poop on the floor.*

*Once the deed is done, all he can do is wait for his humans to come home. And tuck his tail between his legs.*

*The tail never lies.*

At work, your team is the same. Although one would hope they express their anger in slightly less offensive ways. Everyone messes up from time to time, so it's essential to build a culture where people admit it, learn from it and move on.

Even more important is showing your happiness when things go well. It only takes a moment to congratulate someone on a job well done, and the benefits can last a long time. Your colleagues want to look good through your lens. When they feel genuinely appreciated for what they've contributed, they are more likely to do it again because it felt so good.

If you haven't already done so, incorporate a formal recognition program into your process. Acknowledging and showing gratitude for exceptional performance is one of the most motivating tools in your arsenal. Examples can range from a handwritten note of appreciation to a plaque for Employee of the Month, a trophy for Exceeding Customer Retention Goals or a vacation for Salesperson of the Year.

For some, celebrating the many little victories comes naturally. Good, keep it up. But for those who feel odd high-fiving a co-worker who just signed up a new customer, remember everyone likes to see a wagging tail. And it costs you nothing to do it.

- How does your body language show your team how happy you are when they succeed?
- What recognition practices can you implement to encourage your team to celebrate all successes, big and small?

*That's when I fell for the leader of the pack.*
– The Shangri-Las

## THE BIG DOG

If you're the big dog, everyone's looking to you for leadership. While you don't have control over most of the external factors that impact your business, you can influence the way your organization responds to create a competitive advantage and drive positive outcomes.

Business leaders are up to their eyebrows in obligations. Produce results. Deliver on commitments. Develop people. Wow customers.

While there's only one top dog in your organization — the President or CEO — it's likely there are other big dogs. They could be the leader of your department, the general manager of the branch office or the creator of your company's brilliant new idea.

In the dog world, the leader of the pack just evolves. In many cases it isn't the biggest or the strongest. It's the one who shows the right leadership qualities, the dog that the others respect and want to follow.

*The entrepreneurial spirit is alive and well in America. Case in point: the pet daycare industry. This growing niche has emerged to help busy working people not feel guilty about leaving their dogs at home all day.*

*Many dog daycare facilities have separate areas for the large dogs and the small dogs. One evening at one such establishment, just before closing time, there was only one canine left in the small dog area. The worker in charge decided to see how Muffin — a cute little seven pound Papillon — would fare in the room where the Great Danes, German Shepherds, and St. Bernards hung out.*

*It didn't take long to find out. Muffin immediately ran up to Daphne — a one hundred sixty pound Mastiff — and began explaining in no uncertain terms how things were going to go until closing time. Daphne — a lover, not a fighter — liked Muffin's spunkiness. Within minutes Muffin had not only survived the big dog room but had made it her own.*

It's similar in business. Unless you're the owner's progeny, leaders emerge naturally. They win new accounts, solve problems and make good things happen. And as a result, they become the big dog.

That role has to be maintained. Your leadership needs to be demonstrated on a daily basis. Work hard, show integrity and inspire greatness. It isn't always easy but it's what the pack demands.

The leader of the pack is the one who sets the example, disciplines the unruly and figures out how to open the cupboard where the dog treats are stored. He or she needs to know how to set the vision and inspire the team so the company achieves its goals.

The big dog at work needs to strike the balance between Pit Bull and Pekingese, one part strong and decisive and one part lovable and uplifting.

Dr. Paul Hersey of Situational Leadership® fame talked about two main types of power: personal and positional. And the one that's most important for you to be the big dog is personal power.

Personal power, the extent to which you have the confidence and trust of those you lead, is earned from the team. Positional power, the extent to which you can give rewards and punishments, comes from the organization. Develop your personal power in ways that engender respect and you'll be the best in show.

Put a bunch of dogs together for a few minutes and one of them emerges as the leader. It usually isn't the biggest or the meanest or the one with the seventy-five dollar haircut. It's the one with ideas, energy and presence to own the room.

Over time, the same process unfolds at work. People introduce good ideas and help bring them to market with a passion. They use interpersonal skills to persuade, to motivate and ultimately to lead.

There is no one right size for the leader of the pack. Small dogs can be the alpha, too. Young dogs may teach the veterans on the team new tricks. Older dogs may set the traditions that the organization needs to thrive.

Black or white, male or female, young or old: none of these descriptors matter as much as your ability to make good things happen by working with others. If you have the right skillset and a drive to succeed, one day you too can be the big dog.

- How do you earn your role as the big dog with your pack every day?
- Are you more of a "strong and decisive" or "lovable and uplifting" leader and what do you need to do to develop your less natural leadership style?

## GROWLS AND NIPS

Keeping your pack together and moving in the right direction is a lot harder than it looks. First of all, everyone is unique. The Collies like to chase squirrels, Afghans like to chase mice and Terriers like to chase anything that moves. What's a dog to do?

Occasionally things go wrong. When they do, the team leader has to communicate the message properly and in a way so people can learn from the situation and avoid it in the future. In most cases, a simple growl will suffice. If more volume is needed, a bark usually gets the message across. And avoid nips at all costs, as the HR department simply hates dealing with nips.

*Brandy is a Miniature Schnauzer who lives in Grand Rapids. She has an easy-going disposition unless the mailman is at the door or there is cooked meat in the house. This is the story of what happened when they both occurred at the same time.*

*There they were, two burgers being cooked in the kitchen. The smell was driving Brandy crazy and she was in her "one for me, one for you" pre-chow down hysteria. And then there was a sound at the door. The sound of the mailman invading Brandy's home yet again by violating the mail slot. One thing was for sure: Brandy wasn't going to allow the mailman to take her burger.*

*So, she ran to the mail slot and with a ferocity rarely seen in suburban western Michigan she began to fold, spindle and mutilate every piece of mail without any regard whatsoever for its class of postage.*

*She earned the stern lecture she received. After all, the carpet cleaning coupons were shredded beyond recognition. But all was forgiven because the burgers had been protected.*

Everyone reacts to discipline differently, so the leader has to know how much of a correction is needed, all while staying fair and consistent. The trick here is having a keen understanding of your individual team members *before* discipline is meted out.

Delivering the appropriate amount of correction is always a challenge. You have to assess:
- How egregious was the incident?
- How experienced is the employee?
- Is this the first time this has happened?
- Were laws, company policy or safety regulations violated?
- Are you trying to send a signal to the entire team?
- Were you part of the problem?
- Was the original intention noble or nefarious?

It's also important to assess your own behaviors and emotions. If you have a tendency to anger easily, your well-intended message may be clouded by your bubbling-over ire. And while you may think your growl shows you give a darn, those around you will be responding out of fear, not because they were inspired. You don't want others to think you're a rabid dog.

Learn to sense trouble coming the same way the "check engine light" signals an impending problem for your car. Whenever you feel anger boiling over, tell yourself "this is a trigger for me." Bite your tongue and walk away until you cool off and calm down. Count to ten. Breathe in and out deeply. Consider if what you are going to say next is helpful or hurtful. Do something other than lash out. Then refocus on what you really want to accomplish.

Sometimes you may find yourself on the receiving end of a growler or bully. The nip may come in the form of putting down others in public, threatening to eliminate jobs if things don't improve or constantly yelling that things aren't good. This may happen if that person feels their dominant position is threatened by your performance or if they are under enormous pressure.

You own how you express anger and how you practice patience. It doesn't matter if it's someone else's fault. What matters is how *you* react to the situation.

Impatient people can come across as arrogant, insensitive and judgmental. To help maintain composure and improve patience, try these ideas:
- Listen more and interrupt less. Pause before you interject to give people a chance to finish their thoughts.
- Resist the urge to quickly provide a solution. Impatient leaders go from "here's the problem"

to "here's the answer" without ever identifying what success looks like and what the root cause of the problem is. If you don't show others your thought process they won't learn how to solve problems themselves.

- Teach, don't tell. Initially it takes longer but you'll have more engaged and productive co-workers in the long-run.

Your job as a leader is to get results with people and have them feel like they've accomplished something. When things go wrong be judicious, not mean-spirited, in your reaction. After all, a good growl goes a long way.

- What triggers your anger?
- How can you keep your composure while ensuring your message is delivered in a way that allows everyone to move forward?

## YOUR BARK IS WORSE THAN YOUR BITE

Sometimes a well-timed snarl is a very effective management tool. As a supervisor, there are times when you want to make sure your team knows you are not happy with the results. Just make sure you don't take it too far.

*Delilah is the master of the bark. She's a Maltese with a wide range of verbal communication styles that vary from a quiet, low frequency "Is that what I think it is?" warning growl to a frenetic "If I get my paws on you" freak out diatribe.*

*And they all work. Sometimes too well. For example, one of her favorite pastimes is lying near the back door and watching the black squirrels. She never was a fan of the brown squirrels when she lived in Indianapolis and her animosity for their dark-coated brethren stayed with her when she moved to Short Hills, New Jersey.*

*Her problem is that in her exuberance, as soon as the back door opens, she feels compelled to announce she is on a rodent-chasing mission. And while squirrels don't speak dog, they get the message. And skedaddle.*

On occasion we all just want to bark out orders. "Do this!" "Don't do that!" It can feel good to just say exactly what you're thinking. It can also seriously damage relationships. A lack of a filter usually means people hear your negativity loud and clear and don't hear a word you actually said.

You may think you are being candid and direct, but the person on the other side of the conversation may think you're being a jerk. And that can easily happen when you're barking out orders without getting buy-in.

A similar dynamic happens when leaders are constantly arm waving. Saying you're going to make changes if things don't improve is okay, but if you never follow through with action people will eventually quit listening.

If you're constantly barking, people won't grasp the important message you're trying to convey. They will either tune you out or jump frantically from task to task like a flea at a dog park, chasing anything that moves.

*How* you say what you say is just as important as *what* you say. Maybe more.

- Do you frequently bark out orders without getting alignment?
- Is how you say what you say consistent with the message you want to convey?

## SPIRIT OF ADVENTURE

Dogs love to explore. They are always game for a road trip, a hike in the woods or a discovery expedition on a remote stretch of beach. If it's new and different, count them in.

*Dogs love vacations as much as we do. Maybe more. They get to spend extended time with the people they love and they get to smell new things. What a combination.*

*Every spring, Jordan loads up his car and drives from Knoxville to Charleston, South Carolina. Of course he always takes Bruin, his Australian Cattle Dog.*

*Jordan likes to walk along the beach on Isle of Palms, and so does Bruin. When there's no one around he lets Bruin off the leash, free to sniff the sea oats, sand castles and an endless string of holes in the sand created by an army of crabs. Flotsam and jetsam, birds and fish, wind and water.*

*Whether it's hiking in the Smokies, exploring Lake Norris on a pontoon boat or chasing terns on the ocean, Bruin is always up for an adventure.*

In business there are always new things happening. Change is everywhere and it impacts everything. You need to be able to adapt and see change as an opportunity.

So how do you prepare your team for all of the changes coming when you don't know what they are yet? Look for that spirit of adventure. Challenge people to see around corners and embrace change rather than fight it.

Get outside of your comfort zone to learn about, experience and achieve new things. You can start with little things like listening to a new type of music, trying new foods or watching a new channel on TV. At work you want to create an environment where taking some risks is encouraged because that's how people grow and innovation flourishes.

Curiosity is vital to leadership. Urge your team to get close to your customers and question everything. Ask "what if" and "how else could we" questions. Surround yourself with people who are curious about trends and new ideas, as that will help lead you down new paths to prosperity.

Socrates said "The secret of change is to focus all of your energy, not on fighting the old but on building the new." That was Socrates the ancient Greek scholar, not Socrates the black Lab in Waukegan. Either way it's true. You need people who relish the spirit of adventure and pave the way to the bright new future for your enterprise. Curiosity may have killed the cat but it sure helped the dog become an exceptional leader.

- How do you encourage your team to explore opportunities and take calculated risks that could become profitable new avenues for your company?
- What new things are you trying?

## DOG AND PONY SHOW

At some point in your career you'll have to stand up in front of a group of people and talk. It could be as simple as presenting a recap of results in a meeting room or a presentation to hundreds of people at a tradeshow. The ability to persuasively present to a crowd is a highly desirable trait. It also scares the heck out of many people. Luckily, everyone's public speaking skills can be improved.

*The new arthritis drug had cleared all the regulatory hurdles and was finally ready for market. In anticipation of the FDA clearance, an advertising agency was chosen to shoot TV commercials showing how wonderful people felt after taking this breakthrough product. Once the ad was written and approved, the director began casting.*

*One of the biggest challenges was finding a dog to fill a starring role. The storyboards called for a pooch to play on the beach with the commercial's graying but amazingly fit sixty-something year old lead actor. According to the script the dog needed to frolic.*

*After reading the bios of dozens of potential dogs, the director eventually chose an affable hound named Scout. His impressive resume included two TV show cameos, three movie appearances and a web video viewed by 25 million people in France.*

*The talent agent had assured everyone that Scout could frolic his tail off, but when they got to the beach to shoot the scene, the director had an uneasy feeling. This would be a very expensive waste of time if Scout didn't deliver.*

*When the cameras rolled it was clear they were working with a professional. Scout performed up until the director yelled "cut!" and was ready for take after arthritis pain-free take. Lights, camera, frolic!*

It's no secret that public speaking can be very intimidating. Here are some ideas to wow the crowd and reduce the odds that you'll be overly nervous.

Start by asking yourself the following questions:
- Who is my audience?
- What information do I want them to learn?
- How do I want them to feel?
- What next steps do I want them to take?

When creating your presentation, incorporate as much of the following as possible:
- Deliver the most important points in the first two minutes.
- Tell stories and use new facts.
- Speak with conviction using action words.
- Involve the audience.
- Don't read words on the screen verbatim.

Here's some advice to help you pull it all together:
- Practice so you know the material inside out.
- Be yourself. Don't try to be a comedian if you aren't.
- Stand when presenting and make eye contact with everyone in the room.
- Smile and try to relax.
- Dress the part.
- Anticipate technical glitches by having backup equipment.
- Watch how fast you talk.
- Eliminate filler words like "um" and "uh."
- Finish within the allotted time.

A dog and pony show is a special opportunity to raise your leadership profile and shine. Lights, camera, action!

- What can you do to improve your ability to persuade when presenting to groups of people?
- What filler words do you say that you need to eliminate?

## MUTTS

Westminster, the granddaddy of all dog shows, historically only awarded their Best in Show awards to purebreds. The good news is they recently began allowing mutts the opportunity to compete in agility categories. They don't call them mutts, of course. They're "All-American mixed-breeds." Try telling that to an Irish Setter-Australian Wolfhound mix.

There is a lot to be said for purebreds, but they admittedly have some limitations. One is their health, where some dogs suffer from ailments caused by generations of inbreeding.

There is a trend toward mixing some purebreds to create what amounts to a new breed. One popular example is the Golden Doodle, a mix of Golden Retriever and Standard Poodle. The result is a smart, friendly pet that doesn't shed like a typical Golden. The Shih-Poo is another, a mix of the Shih Tzu and Toy Poodle. It's most popular with people who think the name is funny.

America is the ultimate mutt-fest. We are the product of Irish, German, African, French, English, Mexican, Middle Eastern, Chinese, Indian and hundreds of other purebreds. All rolled up into one gigantic kennel we call the United States. We look different from the rest of the world and we think and act differently. Because we are different. Over many generations we've become stronger because of our diversity.

*A couple years ago, when it was time to get a new dog, we did something new. We looked on the internet.*

*Every night for a week we'd Google "Standard Poodle rescue," and one dog kept coming up: Clover. She was living with a rescue family in suburban Detroit. Her YouTube video was adorable. After some phone interviews and a fairly rigorous vetting process — on us, not her — it was all settled.*

*One of the first things we did was take her to our vet, Dr. Bob. It was there that we made a surprising discovery. "She definitely is part Poodle, but I think she has a lot of Portuguese Waterdog in her," Bob declared after a careful examination. Later, as we read up on the traits of Waterdogs, and as we looked for their distinctive characteristics, it became clear he was right.*

*So we had our first mutt. And we wouldn't trade her for the world.*

Best In Show

Business leaders are more aware of diversity than ever before. That's partly because of the desire to avoid discriminatory practices. But the truth is diversity is good for companies because it provides a stronger connection to the marketplace. Diversity fosters different approaches for innovation and problem solving. If all you have in your company are fifty-year-old white guys, you could find yourself out of touch with the interests of women and minorities, as well as baffled by new technology and current trends.

By bringing into your team a diverse mix of people, you will build a better organization. The challenge is always doing it in a way that allows your company to sustain your corporate culture and maintain your standards. Your HR team will help navigate these waters and assist you in hiring and maintaining a fresh and diverse group of the best and brightest.

The challenges businesses face today are multifaceted and daunting. Global competition, mobile technology and changing consumer demands are forcing companies to rethink their strategies. Let's say you work at a business founded by and run by three generations of Doberman Pinschers. If everyone on your executive leadership team also were Dobermans, do you think you'd be totally dialed in to the needs of your Cairn Terrier customers?

*You, in your role as the big dog, have decided to assemble a team to run across a field, explore an old barn, learn what's inside and get back. All without getting spotted. So you do what you do every day: think about the task and decide who to put on the job.*

*How about sending all those hotshot Dachshunds that have been making great things happen? No, upon further reflection you'd likely want a mix of breeds: some that are fast, others with good vision and others that can jump. You'd seek out teamwork, strategic thinking, athleticism, communication skills and fortitude.*

*In other words, you'd want a diverse team.*

The business world is similar. There are some work roles that require supreme intelligence and quick thinking, while others call for brawn and a craftsman's expertise. It is only with the proper mix of skills, behaviors and attitudes that you will create the perfect kennel.

Yes, the mutt is a favorite. That's because Americans are the world's greatest collection of mutts. As a true melting pot for people from around the world, we have a little bit of everything in us. Embracing diversity applies to virtually every successful group or company you can find.

We need all kinds of team members to create a winning pack.

- What is the right mix of people your organization needs to connect to the marketplace and propel you into the future?
- How can you bring diverse thinking into your team?

*The factory of the future will have only two employees, a man and a dog. The man will be there to feed the dog, and the dog to keep the man from touching the equipment.*
– Warren Bennis

## MOTIVATED BY THE VISION

Dogs don't give up when they are on a mission. And they're always on a mission. Whatever they're doing they're always highly motivated.

Put a bunch of dogs together and the motivation factor multiplies.

*Some friends came over for dinner a while ago and brought their two dogs. After our two dogs gave the new canines the welcome sniff they all ran into our backyard and we poured some wine in the kitchen.*

*Fifteen minutes later we wondered what the dogs were up to and discovered to our dismay four very muddy pooches. One of them must have started digging and the others followed suit.*

**Inspirational**

*Had we wanted a big hole in the backyard we would have been very pleased with their progress, but as it turned out, we were not looking to build a swimming pool.*

People will work their tails off if they are properly motivated. Good leaders encourage, coach and demonstrate. They compensate people in a way that is fair, competitive and reflective of their contributions. Through a variety of methods, leaders incentivize people to reach their maximum potential.

The best leaders get everyone to buy in on a higher level objective. Individual power is compounded when people believe they are part of something meaningful. In 1961 President Kennedy said to Congress, "I believe that this nation should commit itself to achieving the goal, before this decade is out, of landing a man on the moon and returning him safely to the earth." That vision helped an entire nation aspire to something meaningful and significant.

The vision doesn't have to be big; it just needs to be aspirational. It's a simple statement that speaks to what the organization wants to be in the future. The vision should connect with every partner on your team so they feel they are contributing something valuable to its realization.

Paint a detailed picture of the vision. Paint it so accurately that if someone were seeing it on a canvas there would be no mistaking what it is. Your vision will determine where you spend your time, talent and resources.

Reinforce the vision regularly at team and one-on-one meetings. It may be developing a cure for cancer, helping North American companies compete and win globally or creating a better everyday life for people. Whatever it is, make sure your team believes in it and knows how they contribute to it.

The pack is the ultimate team. It's the group of people you go to battle with every day. When you've built the best pack that's motivated by a meaningful vision, anything is possible.

- What is your vision at work?
- How do you regularly reinforce your vision so your team is headed toward it versus just going through the motions?

## GO FOR THE GOAL

Few things in life have the power of a goal. It is the direction and target that needs to be achieved for the organization to realize its vision. With clear and realistic goals that are in alignment with the vision, extraordinary things are possible.

Dogs are notoriously poor goal setters. Oh sure, they can achieve some very impressive goals, but dogs aren't naturally big on setting their sights much higher than the pillows on top of the bed.

This is where people come into the picture. As a good leader we help decide what the dog needs. Then together we work toward the desired objective.

> *There's nothing like having a well-behaved dog. One that comes when called, sits when told and doesn't eat the plate of hamburgers when no one's watching.*
>
> *None of this comes easy. But once you've established a goal — "I want Bruno to be obedient" — you can begin to work toward it. That may mean signing up for a class, going every week and practicing sits and stays at night. And with effort, Bruno will learn that when you say sit, it's time to take a seat.*

At work you have different types of goals. Some are for the company, others for a department and some for each individual. Some goals should be long-range, others annual and still others short-term.

To make goals meaningful, you need buy in. Get input from your team on what they think is possible. Stretch goals are good, but they also have to be realistic and motivational. After all, the point is to ultimately achieve them.

Goals that are lofty but achievable are inspiring. They help you and your team run toward something that has real value. On the other hand, goals that are impossible to reach with the resources available can lead to higher levels of stress, demotivation and unethical behaviors. Living under the shadow of impossible goals can produce a toxic, fear-based culture.

Every goal should serve to accomplish something relevant, observable and measurable. The upshot of this is each goal should have a number or date associated with it so you can track progress.

Finally, keep it simple. It's better to have a few goals you can really focus on then to have dozens of goals that are more easily forgotten. Three to five goals is about the right number to bite off. These goals should be connected to your purpose, vision and daily business commitments.

Be sure to put your goals in writing and then develop an action plan on how you will accomplish them. Define exactly what you want, why you want it, the steps that need to happen and milestones or due dates to track progress. Each step you complete will get you closer to success. This is especially critical if the goal is an annual or longer-term initiative.

It can be a challenge getting and keeping the entire team moving toward the objectives. To keep track, make time to review your progress on a monthly, quarterly and annual basis. Your final goal may remain the same, but as outside influences change, the action plan you created may need to be updated. These regular reviews help you stay on-track and allow for course corrections should things go awry. And they often do.

*One of the more amazing management styles is one used in alpine herding. A shepherd whistles commands to a Border Collie up to a mile away to turn the herd in one direction or another. Amazingly, the dog — one of the smartest breeds — properly interprets the signals and moves the flock in the desired direction.*

*The goal is to sell as much wool as possible, so they can't afford to lose a single lamb. Some sheep wander off, so it's the job of the shepherd and the dog to bring them back into the fold. The dog runs, barks and uses strong eye contact to get the desired results. It takes an unwavering commitment — and some sharp shears — to get all that wool to market.*

It's worth noting that whistling is not widely considered to be a good management technique. That having been said, course correcting and herding your team toward the goals you've set work every time.

- Do you have clear, measurable and attainable goals? What are they?
- How do you review and reinforce goals with your team so they always know where they stand and where they're headed?

## CREATURES OF HABIT

Few things will help you succeed more at work than having established routines. People who reach the top rungs of the corporate ladder often have habits that ensure they get the right things done in a timely fashion. Examples are spending an hour every Friday afternoon going through the week's emails to make sure nothing was missed, taking fifteen minutes at the start of every day reviewing yesterday's results and creating a monthly priority list.

Dogs are the masters of routine. They sniff the same trees, grab their favorite play toy when they get home and lay on the same spot in bed. Some of this is because they figured out what they like, but it's also a matter of instinct, a remnant of their primordial past. Vigilance in understanding their surroundings led to survival.

> *Every morning it's the same. When the sun finally climbs above the neighboring house, Shaggy, an Akita, finds his favorite spot at the back of the living room. After an hour his favorite spot is the middle of the room. And a little later it's near the bay window at the front of the house.*
>
> *He loves lying in the sun. Indoors, outdoors...it doesn't matter. Every nap is enhanced by the warm glow of the sun.*
>
> *So when someone wonders where Shaggy is, the first thing they consider is where the sun is in the sky. Odds are they know exactly where to find him.*

If you are a creature of habit, congratulations. That is, if your habits are constructive at work. You may drive some of your co-workers crazy with your obsession with detail, but in the end, things get done.

For those who prefer a freestyle approach, that's fine if you're improvising a guitar solo but not so hot for ensuring the new software hits its go live date. Routines help get work done faster and make things more predictable. All of which helps you deliver superior results on time.

Regardless of your management style, regularly review all your reports, processes and procedures so you can eliminate redundant or unnecessary ones. It's common to see front line workers and managers virtually buried in semi-pointless paperwork and non-essential meetings. Clear the path for your team so they can focus on the things that matter most.

Most of us have a mix of daily things we need to do as well as longer-term, more strategic tasks. Build routines into your time management so you get everything done and build in time for activities that are important to you personally, too. This could include working out before you go to the office or scheduling one-on-ones at the same time every week so you spend less time scheduling and more time meeting.

Organize your day around when you have the most energy. If you're a morning person, schedule your strategic work over your AM cup of coffee. Then plan your administrative tasks, like checking email, at another time. You can also look at scheduling your routines around the days of the week. For example, make Mondays meeting days and Fridays planning days.

Successful people have disciplined habits and behaviors because these habits increase the ability to achieve goals. Start by pinpointing what it is you want to accomplish. Then identify the habits that can help you get them done. Build those habits through repetition into your daily or weekly routines. Enlist the assistance of a co-worker, friend or even an online tool to ensure you stick to your new routines.

- What regularly scheduled habits should you adopt to be more productive?
- How can you add more structure to your workday and workweek so you can focus on the things that matter most?

## ENJOY THE RIDE

One of the more endearing qualities of dogs is their ability to live in the moment. They stay focused on the here and now. They're always fully present, not thinking about what happened yesterday or is going to happen later.

Dogs exude a sense of "let's enjoy this belly rub for as long as we both can." And when it's time to get up, grab a leash and go for a walk, they are fully present for that, too.

Dogs aren't big multitaskers. They do one thing at a time. And they do it with everything they've got.

*Santa Claws was our former white Standard Poodle. Our favorite picture of him is one taken from the front seat looking into the side view mirror. There was Santa, head out the backseat window during a ride, joy radiating from his smiling face.*

*Oh how he loved car rides! Maybe it was the wind in his face, or the sense of adventure. Running down to the pet store for a bag of dog food wasn't too exciting to us, but to him it was pure bliss. He knew how to enjoy the ride.*

Work can be mundane. We get bored doing the same things over and over. We talk to a customer and just go through the motions.

Think about how much more effective we'd be if we replaced cookie-cutter interactions with ones where we were mentally fully present. We'd be thinking about how to help the customer standing right in front of us. And it would be more satisfying than checking email or wondering about the weekend weather forecast.

Multitasking hurts productivity. It lowers your functional IQ, increases error rates and reduces your reflexes. Plus it sends the message to the person standing in front of you that they aren't as important as whatever you're doing on your phone. If you want another reason not to do it, multitasking also makes you feel constantly "on" and overwhelmed. And that can lead to decreased job satisfaction and more difficulties maintaining relationships.

Here are some ideas to reduce multitasking:
- Be disciplined about setting specific times for returning calls, answering emails and checking phone messages.
- Turn off audible and visual notifications about new messages. Leaders should be in a proactive mode, not reactive.
- Track who interrupts you the most, then politely but assertively talk with the perpetrators about toning it down.
- Concentrate on one thing at a time. It may feel like you are being less productive at first, but you'll be surprised at how much more you get done.

- Whenever you find yourself multitasking (or tempted to multitask), stop. Take a few moments to breathe deeply and sit quietly with your eyes closed. These brief breaks refocus your mind, lower stress levels and improve concentration.
- If something urgent comes up, make a note of where you were on your previous activity so you know where to come back to, then shift gears to the new task.
- If you find your mind wandering in a meeting, resist the urge and refocus back on the topic at hand.

Each of us has the ability to change how we see and interact with our work world. Staying focused on the people in front of you is like sticking your head out the window and enjoying the ride. Even if you aren't sure exactly where you're going or how long the drive will be, let your ears flap in the breeze. Enjoy the moment. You'll get wherever you're going faster.

- How have you encouraged and enabled your team to enjoy the ride when doing business every day?
- How often do you multitask and how can you be fully present in every interaction?

## CHASING THE DREAM

Dogs love to chase things. This includes kids on bikes, the neighbor's cat and squeaky toys bouncing down the basement stairs.

*Poppy is an Italian Greyhound who lives in West Hollywood, California. His fenced in backyard contains a swimming pool, nine lemon trees and a jungle gym. None of this excites him very much.*

*Poppy's backyard is also the home to a colony of chipmunks. They, on the other hand, excite him very much. His family is convinced that when his legs twitch when he sleeps he's actually dreaming of chasing chipmunks.*

*If he's outside and spots one of these rodents, he takes off like a rocket. Darting between the swing set, leaping over the chaise lounge and dodging fallen lemons. When there's a chipmunk afoot, nothing will deter this dog from his appointed chase.*

At work, people enjoy chasing dreams, too. And most will do whatever it takes to achieve success once they know what their dream is.

Not everyone knows what they're chasing. To uncover your dreams, make a list of what you really want in life. Here's a guide to help you get started:

- Career — What do you want to build or accomplish?
- Family — How do you want your family to see you?
- Physical — What athletic or health-related goals do you want to achieve?
- Spiritual — How can you practice and grow your beliefs?
- Financial — What do you aspire to achieve?
- Mindset — What old attitudes are holding you back and what new outlooks do you need to embrace?
- Fulfillment — What hobbies or passions do you want to develop?
- Service — How can you help others?
- Intellectual — What do you want to learn?
- Legacy — How do you want to be known?

When you make your own list of the dreams you want to chase, be as specific as possible and include target dates. Then review it periodically. Because while chasing a dream is fun, nothing beats the tremendous sense of accomplishment of actually catching it.

When people are motivated by realizing their dreams they can do amazing things. They are more focused and willing to do whatever it takes to get there. Strive to uncover team members' dreams so you can help them become a reality.

External motivation (like the boss is watching) works. But the best way to get extra effort comes from internal motivation. That's the "I'm going to do it and nothing is going to stop me" type of inner monologue that often comes from knowing what you want to accomplish.

To find your motivational core, go to your "personal why." That's the answer to the question "Why are you doing what you are doing?" It may be to buy a house, provide for your family or to endow a worthwhile organization. Whatever it is, connect to what's really important in your life to motivate yourself at work.

- How can you motivate your co-workers to chase the dreams that will benefit both them and the company?
- What dreams are you chasing?

## PAWS FOR A CAUSE

Dogs have proven themselves uniquely capable of incredible feats of service to humans. There are bomb-sniffing dogs at airports to help keep us safe, police dogs that keep illegal drugs off our streets and search and rescue dogs to find missing people.

Some dogs help people in non-traditional ways. Take courtroom trials when a child has to take the stand as a witness. To make it easier to give testimony, some courts are letting them testify while petting a dog. The child feels safer and is better able to talk about what happened. And of course, dogs love being petted by children.

*Nancy, a ministry worker at a hospital, wanted a dog. Not just any dog, but one that would be able to go to work every day and help console patients. So after an exhaustive search, Nancy adopted a Golden Retriever named Kayla.*

*Kayla had been mostly living alone since her former housemate had passed away. Neighbors would feed her and let her out, but she had very little interaction with anyone. At five years old her future wasn't very bright. Until she met Nancy.*

*The transition into her new life wasn't always easy. At first, Kayla was unpredictable. After she came to love and trust Nancy, she'd cling to her. It was a bad case of separation anxiety. Kayla also had to re-learn how to act around others, and overcome her instinct to be fearful and defensive.*

*Early on, Nancy had her doubts that Kayla would be able to turn the corner. She had a long way to go. But with a lot of love, patience and training, Kayla is now a certified pediatric therapy dog and goes to work at the hospital every day. She brightens the moods of children and virtually everyone else her wagging tail comes in contact with.*

Adversity happens. On a fairly regular basis we are confronted by things that don't go the way we want them to go. You get in the shower and realize there's no soap. A client calls you to say he is very unhappy with the last job you did for him. Your favorite General Manager quits.

There are things in life that can be avoided, and the most successful among us do a pretty good job dodging those potholes. But there are also things that, try as we may, we cannot avoid. And the truth is we are judged more by how we deal with adversity than by how much we avoid it.

Strong leaders guide others past the rough spots to achieve their potential. They put the needs of their customers and their compatriots ahead of their own personal wants. They listen, they empathize and they help.

In a way, each of us plays the role of a therapy dog from time to time. We see a co-worker facing a challenge and we try to assist. Sometimes we can help them fix the problem. Other times, all we can do is just lend an ear and show we care.

- How can you help team members overcome adversity and achieve their fullest potential?
- How would having a dog in your workplace, if only occasionally, provide a therapeutic benefit?

## SHOW ME THE WAY

Service dogs are lifesavers. Some are trained to assist people with disabilities, while others alert people to life-threatening situations like low blood sugar or epileptic seizures.

One of the more remarkable ways dogs help people is by being their eyes. Guide dogs have been helping visually impaired people with mobility for nearly a hundred years and stand as a dramatic example of why the bond between humans and canines is so strong.

*Carl was serving his country in Afghanistan when a bomb exploded in front of him. He awoke in a hospital to the realization that he had lost his sight.*

*The transition from battlefield to civilian world isn't easy for anyone, but for Carl it had its own challenges. Luckily he had one constant: Duchess his guide dog who was his companion everywhere he went. Sure, she'd help him cross streets, but she was much more than just a pair of brown eyes. She was his best friend.*

There are times at work when we need someone to show us the way. Maybe it's how to log into a software program, or how to submit an expense report, or how to diversify your traditional bakery into a line of gluten-free products.

The best leaders are servants. They know leadership is a follower based model. They put their team first, guide them past obstacles and mentor others by teaching them what they know.

Good leaders spread behaviors that breed more good behaviors. They demonstrate how to help others and that servant-leader dynamic becomes engrained in the culture.

They are empathetic to what each member of the organization is going through. There are few more noble contributions then assisting someone who is truly in need.

- If you looked through the lens of others, what would you see and how would that change how you lead?
- How can you adopt a servant-leader approach to supporting your team?

## K-9

Everyone loves K-9 units. They help keep neighborhoods and airports safe. Plus dogs look really cool when they wear their uniform and carry a nightstick.

SERVICE DOG

SEEING EYE DOG

THERAPY DOG

GUIDE DOG

POLICE

POLICE
K-9 UNIT

Improving workplace safety is one of the top initiatives at many companies. A safe environment sends a signal to associates that the company cares about them while it helps hold down costs. That's a win-win.

*It finally happened. We met a dog named Jager who wasn't named after the drink. Not that we'd mock him if he had been, because he's a police dog.*

*Jager is a black German Shepherd who spends his days helping Officer Tim as they patrol the streets of Cincinnati. His discipline, desire to help others and sense of smell are extraordinary. Jager is pretty amazing, too.*

*One day Tim and Jager were called to a burglary. While two other policemen entered the front door, Tim and Jager stationed themselves on the back porch. The criminal heard the noise up front, made a beeline out the back door, ran across the elevated deck and leapt toward the back yard.*

*In the middle of the burglar's finest long jump since high school he was surprised by the sensation of a large dog's jaw chomping down on his leg. This surprise quickly gave way to the painful realization that he had been apprehended by a dog in midair.*

*Jager let Tim handcuff the bad guy. It's good for team morale to keep the human involved.*

Safety is a mindset that starts at the top. Leaders who truly care about each member of their pack send the right signals at every opportunity. They wear hardhats and safety glasses when they walk the plant floor, require safety training and support well-stocked first aid kits throughout their facilities.

The beauty is that a safe workplace is actually an employee benefit that builds loyalty while reducing risk. Companies get back multiple times what they invest in safety programs, so being safe also improves your bottom line.

The newest threat to organizational safety is cyber. One click on the wrong email and your entire business could be in jeopardy. Without proper safeguards, that top secret research project you've spent millions on could wind up in the hands of a competitor. Smart leaders invest in technology and training to minimize the likelihood of data breaches.

Your dog has a zero tolerance policy when it comes to strangers invading your home. As a leader you should have a similar intolerance when it comes to unsafe behavior.

- How do you send the signal that safely performing your job is your highest priority?
- How can you further protect your people, data and intellectual properties?

# Inspirational

**Inspirational leaders are:**
- Motivational
- Encouraging
- Enthusiastic

**Inspirational leaders succeed because they:**
- Help others achieve greatness.
- Paint the picture of what success looks like.
- Communicate with clarity.
- Exude a positive "can do" and "will do" mindset.
- Deal with and overcome adversity.
- Develop routines to get more done.
- Embrace diversity.
- Set lofty but achievable goals and review progress regularly.
- Take calculated risks and explore new opportunities.

**Inspirational leaders are respected because they:**
- Bring high energy and enthusiasm to all tasks to lift spirits and motivate.
- Get buy-in and don't just bark out orders.
- Are patient and know their triggers.
- Discipline and celebrate at the right times.
- Encourage dream chasing.
- Make safety a priority.
- Are servant leaders who don't multitask.
- Make personal sacrifices.
- Are persuasive presenters.
- Are empathetic and understand how others see things.

*It's not the size of the dog in the fight,
it's the size of the fight in the dog.*
– Mark Twain

# Determined

Leadership requires relentless determination to reach your goals. Dogs mix perseverance with a fearlessly resolute attitude.

Combine a sharp focus with a never-give-up mentality and you get someone who is unstoppable. Leaders know they need a team that's fiercely unwavering to succeed.

Determined leaders avoid distractions and say "no" to non-essential activities. They are clear on the goals and resolved to getting results. They start with the end in mind and act with intentionality towards that objective.

Determined leaders just won't give up. They courageously plow forward through the unknown, not letting anything or anyone stop them. When they encounter an obstacle, they work until they figure a way around it. They celebrate the incremental successes along the path to victory.

Determined leaders know how to prioritize, particularly when a crisis hits. They focus on what matters most and finish what they start.

Determined leaders and their teams know *they* control their destinies by their actions. The outside world — including the economy, social trends, politics, environment and competitors — has an impact, but determined leaders completely own their outcomes.

Sometimes it requires sheer will, and sometimes more hard work, but determination is what gives leaders the extra grit and fortitude to see things through to success.

## DOGGEDLY DETERMINED

Our journey at work, and certainly in life, can be challenging. We're constantly hounded by distractions and temptations. There are obstacles in our path blocking us from the greater success to which we aspire. We don't get the promotion we sought, our competitor merges with a strong new partner or new regulations force us to rethink our marketing strategy. The unexpected can happen and it often does.

Dogs are particularly well adapted to dealing with challenges. They still have enough wild in them to make them tough, resilient and persistent. Most notably, when presented with a difficult situation they display their dogged determination to succeed.

*A tornado ripped through Henryville, Indiana and changed Harley's life forever. He is part German Shepherd, part Pug and all dog.*

*Shugs — a mix between German Shepherds and Pugs — are notoriously tough and intelligent. Those attributes were suddenly called into action when his home was ripped apart by the twister. He was disoriented by the devastation and injured. As he tried to find his people, he met a volunteer who gave him food, water and medical attention.*

*She didn't find a collar on Harley, so after a few days of searching in vain for his family she took him to her home near Louisville. The lady was very nice, but Harley missed his people in Henryville. So he left to go find them.*

*His journey was not easy. He didn't know where to go or how to get there, but he was determined to find them. He found his own shelter and food and water. He fought when attacked. And he walked for twenty-four miles.*

*One day he began to recognize the sights and smells. And he came running to the front door of his by-then rebuilt home. There is nothing like the unexpected reunion of dog and family a year-and-a-half later.*

Life will throw you curveballs. You'll get hit by some pitches. You'll get called out on strikes. But the true measure of each of us is how we respond to tough times and bust through obstacles.

You need to act with a sense of urgency. And you need willpower, the self-control to resist and the strength to persevere through challenges and distractions. The competition isn't waiting for you to get your act together, so time is of the essence.

That's why procrastination is your enemy. Don't fill your day with low priority tasks or read emails several times without working on them. Don't delay until you feel like having a difficult conversation and never leave items on your To Do list for weeks at a time.

The first step to not being a dawdler is to figure out why you are hesitating. It could be because the task is unpleasant or overwhelming. Or it could be because you just don't know where to begin.

Here are some tips to help you get moving faster:

- Consciously strive to be more decisive. Collect enough data and input to be able to make a good decision. Then make the decision and move forward. If you wait too long an opportunity may pass you by. Remember: not making a decision *is* making a decision.
- Make a To Do list. Focus on what matters most and don't allow yourself to get sucked into unimportant timewasters.
- Break a larger project into smaller tasks. Sometimes it's easier to dedicate an hour a day over four days than to find an open half day. Plus it helps you build momentum toward completing the project.
- Visualize the completion of the project and how good it will feel to get it done. Enjoy both the journey and the finish line.
- Tell people what you are going to do. Peer pressure is a powerful motivator.
- Reward yourself for achieving milestones as well as finishing.
- Resist temptations like buzzing smartphones and excessive leisure activities.

True determination is not a part-time hobby. When you encounter an obstacle, don't ignore it. Achieving your goals takes daily commitment.

Balance your desire to exude determination with being overly aggressive. Too much determination and you'll come across like you're foaming at the mouth. Too little determination and you'll be known as a docile pushover.

Perseverance is essential because leadership and success in business are long games. Obstacles will litter your path and that's when your resolve to outwork the competition matters most. Only those with a steadfast tenacity will cross the finish line and bring along the entire team.

You may have to fight to prevail. Get rid of any self-doubt you have about reaching your objective no matter how distant it may appear to be.

If you work with people whose negativity is impeding your goals, listen to their concerns and then decide if they are valid. If they are consistent naysayers who complain about everything, limit how much time you interact with them.

You will make mistakes and you may have to try several different approaches until something clicks. But in the end your unflinching resolve will carry the day. True determination cannot be defeated. Ask any Shug.

- In what areas can you improve your perseverance?
- What can you do to get momentum on your most important projects?

## MARK YOUR TERRITORY

Frank Zappa had it right. "Watch out where the huskies go and don't you eat that yellow snow" is some of the best advice ever.

Dogs are masters at marking their territory. It's one of their ways of communicating. It goes something like this:

*Oh look, there's a tree. Let me see who's been by recently. [sniff, sniff] Yep, smells familiar. I better let everyone know I'm still the big dog on this street so I'll send them a quick tweet.*

*Okay, let's get back to our walk. Here, let me get to the front of the pack. Oh yeah, I can only go as far as the leash. No problem.*

*Wait, what's that I smell? There, on the fire hydrant. Hang on a second…it's my old pal Brinkley! Hahaha, you old rascal. Sure, I'll re-tweet that message!*

A dog marking its territory is one thing. But what about humans at work? Can it be done in a way that doesn't end up with you cleaning out your desk and being ushered out of the building by the head of HR? As it turns out there are many ways to mark your territory at work without getting arrested for indecency or vandalism.

Marking your territory is a way to say "this is mine." If you're in sales, the best way to mark your territory is to regularly see your customers. And when you do, be sure to give them one of those coffee mugs with your logo on it. That way when your competitor stops by they'll immediately know this is *your* account.

More importantly, you need to develop a mental attitude that says "I own this." And it works regardless of what it is that you do. Let's say you are in the IT department working on a new software project. You will produce better work and succeed faster if you tell yourself "I own the outcome."

Taking ownership and being accountable can be difficult to do. We all know people who say they're going to do something by a certain date and yet it's always late. And there are those who don't return phone calls or respond quickly to email. If you're guilty of these behaviors, stop doing them because you're creating chaos in the team and losing trust.

When you truly own something you need to follow-up and follow-through to be absolutely sure the job gets done. We live in a world of teams, where many people contribute to a project. That's all well and good, but if you really own the outcome, you are the one ultimately responsible for making sure everyone does his or her part.

As a leader, people are relying on you to do what you said you'd do, respond with input or approval, or contribute your part to the project. Don't let them down. Make personal accountability one of the core values by which you're known. Mark your territory and take ownership of your projects because you are responsible for the outcome.

If something goes wrong, learn from it, apologize and fix it. Even if the root cause stems from someone else's actions. It's what leaders do and your teammates will respect you for it.

There are many ways to mark your territory. Remember you're trying to get a leg up at work, not lift your leg at work.

- What do you own (or are responsible for) at work?
- What can you do to ensure your team knows what outcomes they own?

## ONE TENNIS BALL AT A TIME

We live in a world filled with distractions. Phone calls, texts, emails, people walking into your office: it's hard to stay focused on the things that matter most.

*If you've ever watched dogs undertake a project you know how focused they can be. It doesn't matter what else is going on, they are single-mindedly obsessed with the task at hand.*

*Archie, a Lhasa Apso, is a perfect example. He's a tennis ball aficionado. While he prefers Penn in the high visibility yellow, he is also a fan of the classic Wilson white balls. Sometimes he just feels like going old school.*

*Victoria, who plays mixed doubles twice a week, came home one evening and called Archie's name. There was no response, only a scratching noise coming from the living room. As she approached the sound it became clear what was going on.*

*There, lying awkwardly on the floor, was Archie. Or at least his back half. He had squeezed his head and front legs under the sofa where he desperately pawed in vain to reach his favorite tennis ball.*

*It's a good thing Victoria was there to free the ball. Archie might have changed strategies and decided to burrow down through the couch.*

At work we measure things. The number of tons of steel plate we made during an eight-hour shift, how many scoops of ice cream we served in a month or the number of full service oil changes year over year. We measure things because it keeps us focused on what we need to do. What gets measured gets done.

Work isn't always fun. That's why they call it work. But we can make it more enjoyable by focusing and staying in the moment. Make every ice cream cone like it's going to be photographed for the cover of a magazine. Because each sundae matters, each milkshake counts and each banana split gets you closer to the goals you and your company have set.

How can you sharpen your focus? Make a list of your priorities and then focus on those that matter most. Be brutally honest and rank the importance of each item. Then be disciplined in how you spend your time, devoting the vast majority to those elements that will have the greatest impact on you and your company.

Prioritizing is not just for the mega issues. It also cascades from strategic objectives to day-to-day activities. The hourly question of "what should I do next?" should always be answered by thinking first "what is my highest priority?" Think of time as money. If you spend it on an activity, what aren't you able to do?

Making conscious strategic decisions is one of your most important activities. Don't allow daily distractions to take your eye off the ball. Allow time for unanticipated events by never scheduling more than 80% of your day. Beware of time zappers like emails, social media, phone calls and texts. One strategy to manage your time is to set aside certain blocks of the day to do administrative tasks and other times to focus exclusively on your top strategic initiatives.

Attack your priorities by shutting your door, turning off the phone and closing your email. This undistracted focus will help you concentrate on the heavy lifting and get the job done faster. Always do your hardest work when you are at your maximum capacity. Then reward yourself with a short break.

If you're ready to take on extra structure, try creating a priorities document that is segmented into three columns: quarterly goals, monthly priorities, and weekly activities. Everything on your weekly list should help you achieve your monthly priorities and everything on the monthly list cascades up to realizing your quarterly goals. Every week assign how much time you think it will take to do each item on your weekly list. Then shorten the time by 25% to force efficiency. Label each item with an A, B or C priority and do the A's first. You'll get more done in less time.

Keep your focus on what needs to be done to get and keep customers, and what you can do to help achieve the company's vision. After all, you can chase the tennis ball and do a lot of activity with a tangible outcome. Or you can chase your tail and run in circles.

- How do you ensure you're focused on what matters most and not just doing busy work?
- What is the order of your most important priorities and how do you ensure you invest the appropriate amount of time in each area?

## BOW-WOW WORK ETHIC

Somewhere along the line "work like a dog" became a bad thing. It's a phrase people use when they complain about working too hard. That's unfortunate, because we have a lot we can learn from dogs when it comes to effort.

Broadly speaking, there are three types of people in this world: those who consistently work hard, those who occasionally work hard, and those who are just plain lazy. As you might imagine, those who consistently work hard tend to succeed at a far greater rate than those who only occasionally or never do it.

This isn't to say that emotional intelligence, knowledge, executive presence, education, personal connections and experience don't play huge roles in how successful a person becomes. They do. The point here is simply this: each of us has been dealt a certain hand in life. The biggest determinant of success in the future is how much effort we exert.

There are many reasons why some people work harder. It may just be how they are wired, or they may be highly motivated by a goal, or they may even have a fear of failure. That's other people. Let's talk about *you*.

You are the only one who is really in control of you. And you control every choice you make. One choice you make over and over every day is how hard you work. It's safe to say most people could kick it up a notch. Good things tend to happen to people who put in the effort. Wouldn't it be nice if those good things happened to you?

*Dogs are wired to work hard. The average Terrier never has to psych itself up to chase squirrels. He goes outside, sees a squirrel and his nature takes over. Luckily for squirrels, Terriers can't climb trees or jump from branch to branch. But don't tell that to a Terrier.*

The difference between successful and very successful people is often persistence. Thomas Edison invented one thousand unsuccessful light bulbs before he finally got it right. Most people would have given up after half a dozen attempts. Dogs don't give up easily and will hound you until they get what they want. If something is worth achieving, commit to pursuing it tirelessly until you succeed.

Working long hours and making personal sacrifices won't guarantee success. But combine them with becoming more productive and you've got a winning formula. Prioritize your time, invest your energy wisely and don't procrastinate. Start your day accomplishing a goal, like going for a run, and then work to keep the momentum flowing.

There is a difference between working hard and working too hard. If you are energized by your work and not ignoring other aspects of your life (like family, health, play and spirituality) then working hard is a positive. If work completely takes over your life, get ready for trouble.

Working eighty hours a week is not a badge of honor. Achieving success is. Don't cram your schedule to the point that your life is unfulfilled. Eliminate unimportant activities so you can concentrate on the things that really matter.

Invest the time to understand why some team members consistently under produce. Maybe it's a training or resource issue, or perhaps it's a temporary personal matter. Establish clear expectations about output and effort. Make sure your employees know that your intention is to help them and the entire team succeed.

Set the example with your work ethic and others will follow.

- What sacrifices do you need to make to achieve your goals and boost your work output?
- How truly persistent are you in going after your goals and how do you integrate both work and home priorities?

## LICK YOUR WOUNDS

Dogs are not complainers. It takes a lot of pain to prompt even a whimper. And if they do injure themselves, they take matters into their own paws and lick their wounds. We admire dogs for their self-reliance and lack of whining.

This process of self-treating has its upside. It removes dirt so the wound can heal faster. But it is not a cure all. Serious cuts and gashes require medical attention.

*Otis is a Dalmatian-Corgi mix. The first thing you notice about him are his ears. They are magnificent. They are large. And they stand up and almost wave at you when he says hello.*

*The second thing you notice is he likes to chase deer in the woods behind his house. You infer this from the fact that he is often licking his wounds caused by the thorns of the rambling rose bushes that line the yard. It's just a minor occupational hazard and nothing a few laps from his pink tongue can't take care of.*

There are two types of injuries people incur at work: physical and emotional. If you get a paper cut on the job you go to the medicine cabinet, clean it up, put a bandage on it and get back to work. If you sustain a more serious injury, you go to the clinic or hospital.

The more common injuries on the job are the unseen emotional scars. A mean joke by co-workers, being excluded from a critical decision or an angry outburst by a supervisor can hurt more than a paper cut. And take longer to heal. As the leader, you set the tone of your workplace. If you want to attract and retain the best employees in your field you need to be vigilant about eliminating workplace caused emotional wounds.

We all have a tendency to lick our own wounds, to self-diagnose our injury and prescribe the right medicine to treat it. A salesperson who is struggling may choose to read a how-to book to turn around his or her fortunes, and that's admirable. But it may not be enough. Sometimes we need to ask others for help. And if you reach out to others, ask for two specific ideas you can start doing right away. And then start doing them.

A leader has to be tough. You have to bounce back from adversity and accept constructive criticism with aplomb. When we own up, apologize and fix mistakes promptly, others usually feel good about the experience. Quickly regroup and put yourself on an upward trajectory by incorporating all the painful lessons you just learned.

Sometimes, the injury is not as bad as you may think. Give yourself permission to forgive yourself or the person who inflicted the wound. Work on improving the situation to avoid re-injury. And move on.

- How can you discover what wounds you need to heal?
- How do you handle constructive criticism and implement those ideas?

## LET SLEEPING DOGS LIE

Leadership is an art, not a science. The most effective leaders know what technique to use at the right time to get the desired result. The "let sleeping dogs lie" approach is a way to get past difficult situations. Essentially you make the executive decision to not reopen a contentious topic because the downside outweighs the upside.

*Alfie is a Boston Terrier who lives in Tampa. Yes, she roots for the Red Sox. Unless they are playing the Rays, of course.*

*Like most dogs, she likes to sleep. What's notable about her is if she's startled when awakened, she has a rather snappy disposition for a few moments. And by "snappy" we mean downright snarly, surly and ill-tempered.*

*To a visitor at her house, this can be a little disconcerting. "Oh look…isn't Alfie so cute when she's sleeping" can quickly turn into "AAAHHH! She almost bit me!"*

As a leader, your job is focusing on the future, not dwelling too much on the past. The real trick is knowing the difference between an unresolved issue that could cause problems in the future and one that would serve little purpose in readdressing. Once a decision is made, move forward and don't second guess yourself.

You've probably been in a meeting where a decision was made and then someone keeps advocating for a different direction after the fact. It's a great way to get the team misaligned and to foster discord. Sometimes for the good of the team, you just need to let sleeping dogs lie.

- Are you able to let sleeping dogs lie or do you feel compelled to advocate for your position even after a decision has been made?
- What things — ideas or decisions — do you need to let go of?

## BACKED INTO A CORNER

A dog may bare its teeth when backed into a corner. It's a "fight or flight" instinct that takes over, and with no way to flee, it's time to fight.

As a leader, one of the most difficult situations is when you get backed into a corner. The best advice: try to avoid being put in that position. Nothing pretty ever happens.

But when you do find yourself in an undesirable situation, listen to what the other person is saying and try to understand his or her point-of-view. When you listen, you may learn something new. Try to align with the other person on what would be a good outcome and together create a plan to get out of that corner.

*A mother Chihuahua was out for a walk with her litter of six puppies. Suddenly she found herself at the back end of an alley with a big, mean cat coming right at them. There was no way to escape and the puppies were petrified.*

*The quick-thinking mother dog boldly stepped toward the cat and in the fiercest voice she could muster said "meow, meow, meow!" The cat was so startled it turned and fled.*

*The mother looked at her puppies and said, "Now you know the importance of learning a second language."*

You can get backed into a corner when a customer or co-worker asks you to do something you can't (or shouldn't) do. Stand your ground and help the other person see the situation from your perspective. And always do the right thing, even when no one is watching.

It's easy to get angry and defensive when you're cornered. Here are some better ways to respond:
- Try to see the situation through the other person's eyes.
- Give yourself time to respond. Don't push "send" on a hastily written email.
- Keep it professional. Don't take things personally and don't lash out.
- Stay focused on what you want the outcome to be.

When you feel backed into a corner, have a go-to response that buys you time and lets emotions simmer down. A good message to have ready is "Thank you for your input. You've given me something to think about." You could also use "Meow, meow, meow," but that usually only works with cats.

- How can you avoid being backed into a corner?
- Do you try to understand what the other person is saying and see the situation from their point-of-view?

## SHAKE IT OFF

Some dogs love the water and some don't. For those who do, nothing beats bounding into a lake in the summer to chase a wave or fetch a stick.

And when back on dry land, dripping wet, they just shake off the water. It's an amazing thing to watch, the way they whip their bodies back and forth, spraying water everywhere and speeding up the drying process. And when they're done they just move on.

*Rasta is a Portuguese Waterdog who lives in Fernandina Beach, Florida. Much to her chagrin, she is afraid of the water. Her family members thought they could turn things around by taking her to a friend's pool and watching their dog enjoy the water.*

*It was a hot summer day when Rasta and family arrived at the other home. There they discovered Maggie, a Chocolate Lab, gleefully jumping into her pool. Rasta took one look and headed for the shade. So one of her family members picked her up and walked into the shallow end of the pool. There was a look of terror in Rasta's eyes as they slowly got wet. She fought like a lobster trying to avoid a boiling pot of water.*

*After a few seconds she broke free of the grasp and scrambled up the stairs and out of the pool. She looked back at the family member as if to say "just because I'm a Waterdog doesn't mean I like water!" Then she shook it off, spraying everyone nearby, and was ready to enjoy the afternoon. Over near the food, not the pool.*

Many people struggle to shake things off at work. If a co-worker complains that we forgot to give him the data he needed to finish a report, or a customer dislikes how we handled a problem, that negative memory can hang with us for a long time.

It goes both ways. Sometimes other people do things that get under our skin. We often take it personally. But if you shake things off, you can rebound from most setbacks quickly and move on.

It's easy to wallow in misery. If you find the right compatriots you can whine and moan for months or even years. But it won't do you — or them — any good.

This isn't to say we should ignore all bad things that happen at work. Far from it. The easiest trick is to pivot from what you *don't* want to what you *do* want.

Trust other people's positive intentions. It's highly unlikely your co-workers want to mess up a project, so assume everyone on your team is trying to contribute. Pivot from the negative (we lost a big opportunity) to the positive (let's win the next one). If you give off positive vibes to your team, you'll increase effectiveness and productivity. On the flip side, negative vibes produce distrust and suspicion.

Bad things happen. When they do, we have to be resilient and figure out ways to get past them. How we do that is often the most lasting impression we make on co-workers and customers. So pivot and shake it off.

- How much do you think about past setbacks versus focusing on future goals?
- How are you steering yourself and others to run towards what you want instead of away from what you don't want?

## BALL IN THE LAP

Most pooches are natural marketing geniuses. They make you acutely aware when they want something and then persuade you to act.

> *Take the old ball in the lap move. There you are, sitting on your sofa watching TV after a long day at work. The next thing you know there's a tennis ball in your lap and your dog sitting in front of you, staring into your eyes, smiling. You try to ignore the request for a game of fetch. Seconds later you feel a nudge and see your dog pushing the ball toward you with his nose.*

> *Just as you are softening to your dog's persuasion you are drawn back to the TV show. After all, they are down to only two bachelorettes and this is the final date with the girl's mother acting like she's the waitress at the restaurant.*

> *There's another nudge, followed by a paw on your leg, followed by a smile. And you happily relent.*

Sales and marketing are all about finding a way to persuade. To get someone to see a situation your way requires an emotional connection, a mutually beneficial outcome, timing, placement and repetition. Watch a sales and marketing pro in action and they make it look easy. They are wired for what they do, they have honed their skills and they produce results.

Selling isn't just for the salesforce. Every single person in your company can have a positive impact on the company's top line. How customer service answers the phone, the way your field techs complete their jobs and how accurately billing statements are produced all contribute to the likelihood that a customer will come back to purchase from you again.

Every position at work requires persuasion skills. Maybe you need to persuade others to use your new Customer Relationship Management system, invest in a new innovation or keep using the same accounting firm. Most conversations have a persuasive component to them. The ideal balance is to persuade while not being obnoxious by overselling and wearing out the other person.

Persuasion is often confused with selling. But it's more than that. It's really about getting alignment on what the goal or outcome is. Unless you're a lone wolf — technically a dog's close relative, by the way — you need to get results through other people. And that means you need to persuade effectively.

You may not be able to persuade someone the first time you try, but don't give up. It may take multiple conversations to align someone with your perspective. Think like a chess player and plan multiple moves ahead, each time finding a different way to convey your message.

You and your entire company are building relationships with customers and prospects every day. It's just as likely to happen at your kid's soccer game as at a quarterly customer review. Equip and empower your team with the knowledge needed to make every interaction persuasive enough to help move the entire organization forward.

- How do you align goals with what's really important to the other person?
- How often do you stop trying too soon in the process?

## PICK OF THE LITTER

Building an exceptional pack at work doesn't happen by accident. You might get lucky and your next applicant is Lassie or Rin Tin Tin. But more often than not it's up to you to develop the team you want.

The selection process takes forethought and effort. While winners are attracted to winners, the truth is everyone is attracted to winners. With discipline and patience, you can build an amazing team.

**Determined**

It isn't just random luck that we form close bonds with our dogs. The reason is simple: in most cases we made a conscious decision to get that specific pooch. We went to the shelter or breeder, or searched on the internet. We looked at them and played with them. At the end of the selection process we chose that specific dog, not its brother or sister. Why? Because this process is critical to you and your dog bonding for life.

*We've been a Standard Poodle family for years. When one passed away a few years ago, we knew it was time to get another puppy.*

*So we started to do our research. We found a dog rescue an hour away that had a new litter, so off we went to begin the interviewing process. Of course, we took our twelve-year-old Standard Poodle so she could conduct her own one-on-ones.*

*The rescue organization was based at an idyllic farm with open fields and rustic barns. And of course there were dogs everywhere, each one more adorable than the next.*

*Then the job got harder. After an hour of interaction, we had to choose between two cute little puppies that seemed very similar. In the end, one of them had eyes that reminded us of our first dog and a look that said "I am really smart." He also kept following us when we took a few steps away. He seemed to really like us.*

*But the final interview was the one that sealed the deal. It was when our twelve-year-old dog played with the puppy. Just seeing both tails wagging told us everyone was in agreement: this was the right dog for our pack.*

One of the most important things you can do as a leader is to build a top performing team that shares your core values. The only way to assemble the best team is with a thorough and at times painstaking hiring process.

Excessive turnover is one the biggest drags on a company. When you make a bad hire you waste enormous amounts of time and money. Even worse, having the wrong people wearing your uniform can cause damage to your product quality and reputation.

You can reduce the likelihood of bringing on the wrong person with the right hiring process. With the vast majority of turnover caused by poor hiring decisions, it's important to make educated decisions.

Start by making a list of exactly what competencies and characteristics you want. Then create a good interviewing and assessment process. Get everyone in the team involved. You wouldn't get a new dog without consulting your family, so don't go it alone when you're looking for a new hire. Here's a checklist:

- Instill a clearly defined hiring process that is used with all hires.
- Identify exactly what qualities and competencies you are looking for with each position.
- Consider the skills, behaviors, motivators and values needed for the job to ensure the person is a fit with both the role and your company's culture. Assess each candidate for those attributes with an EEOC-compliant assessment tool that's backed by an adverse impact study.
- If the person has the right behavioral mix, then consider their education, experience and references.

By incorporating a rigorous hiring process you will upgrade the quality of your most valuable resource: your team.

- What steps do you need to add to your hiring process to ensure you get the pick of the litter?
- Do you have an assessment program and does it measure behaviors, motivators, competencies and culture fit?

## OLD DOGS & NEW TRICKS

First of all, don't call them "old dogs" or your HR department will be all over you. And yes, you can teach experienced dogs new tricks...just like veteran employees.

The root of the adage is that change is hard for most of us, no matter our age. If we've been doing something in a certain way for a long time and then suddenly we're supposed to do it another way, that presents a challenge.

## Determined

*For some reason, dogs love riding in cars. Maybe it's because they can hang their heads out the window and catch the wind in their faces. Maybe it's because they are going somewhere, which makes it an adventure. Or maybe it's because if they throw up in the back seat, someone else will clean it up.*

*In any case, Buttons, an eleven year old Sheepdog, was used to riding in the back seat of his family's small SUV. He had the pattern down: the driver would open the back door, he'd survey the situation with a couple assertive sniffs, then jump in.*

*Life was good. Then his family got a new two-door coupe. It had a back seat, but to get in it, someone had to slide the front seat forward. This left a small and somewhat awkward opening for Buttons, an eighty-five pound ball of fur. It wasn't the same as the old car.*

*Buttons was bound and determined to learn a new trick. He was not going to let a completely unfamiliar door stand between him and wherever the heck it was they were going. So after a cautious examination of the new arrangement he boldly jumped in. He smiled all the way to the post office.*

Continuous learning is a mindset that attracts people who want to acquire new skills. As quickly as the world is evolving, promoting a culture that embraces change could be a powerful competitive advantage for your company. It can give every member of your team – rookies and veterans alike – the confidence needed to adapt to the ever-changing business landscape.

If your business is like many others and is facing a potential workforce shortfall, make a note of the fifty-five-to sixty-four-year old demographic. It's one of the fastest growing age groups and one where additional training is especially critical.

Just as importantly, there's a lot that older workers and younger workers can learn from each other. Baby Boomers are different from Generation Xers, who are different from Millennials. Tapping into each generation's strengths is critical to better serving your customers. Perhaps your more seasoned associates can teach the pups about loyalty, hard work and experienced-based skills. And maybe your younger workers can teach white-bearded dogs about social media, fashion trends and how to post videos from the mosh pit at Lollapalooza.

The happiest pet people are those who have devoted considerable time to training. That's because they know if they put in the work up front, their dog will understand their expectations and be a wonderful companion for many years to come.

And while they are at it, they also form a critical bond between human and canine during training. This connection is forged in consistency, discipline and love. It establishes trust and helps your dog settle in to its new life as a part of your family.

*The first day of school is always a bit disconcerting. Even when it's doggie obedience school. Will Rover get along with the other students? Will the teacher be nice? Will Rover pee all over the classroom?*

*It didn't take long to find out. Rover immediately marked his territory, temporarily embarrassing his family. And then they learned that all the dogs did it. It was Puppy 101, after all.*

*Sit. Stand. Stay. Shake. Heel.*

*Rover loved school. Maybe it was getting out and meeting other dogs. Or maybe it was spending quality time with his family. Or maybe he actually enjoyed learning new tricks. Whatever the reason, when combined with plenty of practice at home, it wasn't long before he won a blue ribbon. True, they gave out a lot of blue ribbons, but Rover got one of them. His family was so proud of him at graduation.*

Training is critical to your new recruits at work, too. It sends positive signals that you want them to succeed and they are an important part of the future. Training is how you communicate information needed for them to achieve their utmost potential. It builds confidence, and few things will enable people to grow and develop faster than believing in themselves.

Too often, dogs are brought home because they are cute, and then returned because of their unwanted behaviors. This is just like how some people are hired because it looked like they had the right experience. Those same hires may be fired or not promoted because of their misaligned behaviors and attitudes that were not identified prior to employment. Behaviors always predict results, so teach acceptable behaviors. Get your senior leadership team involved with new employees so they can imprint the company's values and culture.

Training is done for many reasons. It opens access to new opportunities and strengthens existing skills. Here are some tips to maximize your training experience as a learner:

- Participate fully. As Ben Franklin said, "Tell me and I forget, teach me and I may remember, involve me and I learn."
- Be open to learning. Even if you think you know the material, look for the one thing you didn't know.
- Stay focused on the topic at hand.
- Have fun, as the more you enjoy the process the deeper the learning sinks in.

The amount of energy put into anything is almost always the key determinant of how successful the output is. If you put the effort into training, you'll be able to teach *all* your dogs new tricks.

- What are you doing to ensure all your employees — both old and new — learn at least two new tricks a year?
- In what ways are you personally involved with hands-on training?

## IN PRAISE OF PRAISE

One of the most popular concepts in training is called "do's." The idea is simple: show them what you want them to do. Then when they actually do it, you reward them.

A variation on this approach is the "treat method" of training. This is where the dog earns a snack every time they do something right. While it's a fun and pleasant way to begin the training process, we've always thought it was the brainchild of some marketing genius to boost sales of cheesy bacon jerky snacks.

Another potentially more effective method is the "praise method." When you are training your dog to sit and they actually do it, you praise them wildly.

*Good boy, Duke! You really know how to sit! Wow, that was amazing and incredible! I'm so proud of you!*

*Woof, woof, bark.*

*Okay, okay...we'll stop. We didn't realize we were embarrassing you in front of your dog friend, Lulu.*

Dogs love praise. It makes them feel good about themselves and what they've accomplished. And it works. Show them what makes you happy and it will foster a repeat of that same behavior.

Of course, people are the same. When you praise someone, he or she will want to experience that same uplifting feeling again, so it reinforces good behaviors.

You want people to be motivated by your leadership and the way you make them feel, not just the material things you can give them. Otherwise they'll leave the moment someone else offers them more money. Giving praise increases feelings of pride, happiness and engagement. People who feel sincere appreciation for a job well-done are more motivated to do an even better job.

Some typical reasons why leaders *don't* praise are:
- They're just doing their job. Isn't that what they get paid for?
- I never got kudos for doing that job so why should others get them?
- I'm too busy to stop and say something positive.
- I'm not that kind of a person. If I start praising people they'll think I'm a phony.

Doggonit those are weak excuses. Praising gives closure to a job well done and is a great idea. And here's the best thing about it: it's free! While it costs you nothing, it means the world to the other person. Need another reason? Praise reinforces a positive culture and helps achieve results.

The best leaders actively look for opportunities to give a thumbs up to someone. At the end of each day, think about someone who deserves recognition and then give it. At the end of the week, take time to write three people a handwritten note about something they did that helped you or the company. Walk around the office at 4:00 in the afternoon and ask what each person has done to make a positive difference that day.

Here's a pro move: when you give praise in a team meeting, be specific about what behaviors you are praising. "Margaret did a great job" is nice. "Yesterday, Margaret came up with a brilliant solution to the Acme problem and saved us time and money" is even better.

You can give praise in the form of short positive statements to yourself, too. Use affirmations anytime you want to envision a positive outcome. When you praise yourself, your confidence, productivity and self-esteem will increase. It's that extra push you may need to keep doing or finish something. Some examples of self-praise include:

- I can do this!
- I have the experience needed for this project!
- No one is better prepared to succeed at this than I am!

Don't hold back. Praise, praise, praise!

- How and how often do you show others you appreciate them and their contributions?
- What affirmations do you say to yourself on a regular basis?

*There are times when even the best manager is like the little boy with the big dog, waiting to see where the dog wants to go so he can take him there.*
– Lee Iacocca

## HOWL NO

As you can imagine, the flip side of "do's" training is "don'ts."

"Don't" training is something else altogether. If you're trying to teach your dog not to relieve himself in the house, treats and praise aren't going to cut it. You need a different approach. Enter the "correction method," known to many as the "be direct, let them know you're frustrated and rub their nose in it" system. When combined with praise for actually doing something right — like going to the bathroom outside — it can work pretty well.

*Sadie wants to be a good girl. She really does. But, as any Shih Tzu knows, sometimes it's hard.*

*For example, there are times in the middle of the night when she makes the choice to go down to the basement to pee instead of waking someone up to go out. That's not good.*

*Her family usually recognizes this has happened when they smell something amiss downstairs. That combined with a wet spot on the carpet.*

*At that point, Sadie usually remembers what she did and tries to hide. So they take her by the nape of the neck and more or less drag her to the crime scene. There she is informed that a forensic team has done extensive DNA testing and she was a match. She does not like being accused, convicted and sentenced. But the swiftness of the justice system helps to remind her that she should not do it again.*

*Her rate of recidivism is decreasing. The carpet cleaners aren't happy, but Sadie's family is.*

"Rub your nose in it" may sound harsh and it's not meant to be mean. It is simply intended to show someone where they're off track. Sometimes you have to make it clear that you are not happy with specific behavior or results. Punishment is powerful so it has to be done judiciously. If done too often it creates an environment of fear, and that never works in the long run. Your goal is to create the right conditions for success, not one fraught with pitfalls.

Part of the trick is to remove the ability for negative behavior to occur in the first place.

In the case of a dog peeing in the house, maybe all that's needed is to close the door to the basement. Leaders need to create the environment where people can and want to be successful. And leaders need to look at themselves for where they may be part of the problem.

Corrective measures need to be balanced with showing how to do something right. It's telling, not yelling.

Some leaders are uncomfortable giving negative feedback. If you are one of those leaders, then you are empowering the negative behavior to continue. And that inevitably will hurt profitability, productivity, engagement and retention. You get what you accept.

When talking with someone who has fallen short, start by positively aligning on the objective. Then be specific about what they did or did not do. Explain what the negative impact is. Guide them through the next steps toward a solution. Be clear about your expectations and focus on what you want instead of what you don't want.

Optimism is a wonderful trait for leaders as long as they don't turn a blind eye toward problems. A Pollyannaish attitude can lead to not catching small problems before they become big ones.

There are times when praise is the right approach and there are times when a correction is needed. You should decide which to use based on performance. The rule of thumb is praise if they are performing and give a correction if they are not.

Give your praise or correction as close to the act as possible. This way the connection is strong between their action and your reaction. The message is very muted if it takes months for you to weigh in, so don't wait for the annual performance review to tell someone how they're doing.

The most powerful messages are those the big dog sends with his or her example. Actions speak louder than words, so make sure your actions support the dos, not the don'ts.

- How do you demonstrate when you are displeased with performance?
- How do you need to balance your mix of praises and corrections?

# Determined

**Determined leaders are:**
- Persistent
- Disciplined
- Accountable

**Determined leaders succeed because they:**
- Never give up. Ever.
- Assemble a championship team using a rigorous hiring process.
- Keep their list of goals short and make them priorities.
- Focus on what matters most and avoid distractions to get more done faster.
- Continuously train and learn.
- Ask for constructive criticism and implement improvement ideas.
- Apologize and forgive.
- Concentrate on the future, not the past.

**Determined leaders are respected because they:**
- Pivot from the negative to the positive.
- Share their fierce resolve with their team.
- Lose negative baggage and shake off minor setbacks.
- Persuade by aligning goals to what's important.
- Own the outcome.
- Try to understand other perspectives.
- Praise the good and correct the bad.
- Build confidence in themselves and others.
- Are decisive and act with urgency.

*I'm running with the pack, never looking back.*
– Bad Company

# Observant

Dogs are highly observant, constantly searching for more information. They use all their senses, watching and sniffing and listening for meaning. Then they make their decisions.

In a world where information is plentiful and fast changing, only those leaders who are dedicated to soaking it all in and assimilating it into a cohesive strategy will prevail.

Observant leaders sense things others miss. They feel momentum shifts and read body language. They look for and identify patterns because they are willing to see things from a different perspective. They listen intently and act when something doesn't smell right. Observant leaders aren't easily distracted and are always aware of their surroundings. They knit together disparate pieces of information to help them draw informed conclusions.

Observant leaders are curious about what they are seeing, hearing and feeling as well as what they are *not* sensing. That curiosity drives them to ask questions in search of deeper meaning.

Observant leaders are self-aware. They know how their emotions and actions affect other people. They know their strengths and weaknesses. They self-regulate themselves based on what their emotions are telling them, helping them to project consistent, emotionally intelligent behaviors.

Observant leaders spot problems before they become serious issues and identify opportunities before the competition does. They are known as people who pay attention and are fully present in the moment. They notice the little things.

*If a dog will not come to you after having looked you in the face, you should go home and examine your conscience.*
- Woodrow Wilson

We live in a world of sensory overload. In a five-second slice of life as we drive to work our phone vibrates in our pocket, we check our rearview mirror, the radio blares, we sip coffee and smell the bag of bagels.

Our senses give us important clues to what's going on around us. But many of us have become desensitized. The best leaders look for clues, listen for hidden meaning and sniff out opportunities. You'll be rewarded for having sensed early what others only later discover.

## BELLY RUB

Dogs like to be petted. As luck would have it, we like to pet them. No wonder we get along so well.

> *Zeus is a Pomeranian, and like his namesake, he's king of his domain, which is an apartment on the upper west side of Manhattan. He likes strolls in Central Park, playing with a green toy mouse that squeaks and the cute little Cavalier King Charles in 6B.*
>
> *And he likes to snuggle. When his family comes home from work, Zeus hops up on the sofa next to them and curls up. He likes the feeling of closeness while getting a head and back massage. He reciprocates with black tongue kisses, his specialty. Life is good.*

A kiss on the head, a belly rub that makes one leg shake uncontrollably, scratching behind the ear: none of these are recommended for you to do with your co-workers. But your dog loves it.

Physical contact is vital to our wellbeing. Touch is a basic way to communicate and connect with others. We use it to show compassion, build confidence and send encouragement.

Our sense of feel is acute. At work, we shake hands. We examine a fabricated part for fit and finish and judge the quality of a bolt of fabric. We create a new app and then play with it to get the full user experience. As often as possible, put yourself in the customer's shoes so you can judge how your product or service feels to them.

There are plenty of human resource department restrictions when it comes to touching in the workplace, and they're there for good reasons. But there are many times when a pat on the back or a hug is appropriate. We need to connect and bond with our co-workers by celebrating the victories and mourning the losses. Don't be afraid to reach out to someone. Just watch out for those belly rubs.

- How does your body language show how you really feel?
- How often do you high-five co-workers?

## ANIMAL INSTINCTS

Most things in life are learned: how to hit a curveball, how to drive a car with a stick shift and how to fill out an expense report. But there are some things we just *know*, like recoiling from a hot stove or feeling anxiety when up on a tall ladder.

Puppies come into the world with a full arsenal of instincts to help them survive. Included among them is their unwavering defense of those closest to them.

*Frasier is half Lab, half Doberman and all dog. Loving, fearless and playful, he's the perfect dog to take on a hiking adventure.*

*On his first expedition in the Great Smoky Mountains National Park, Frasier led the way along the trails toward the campsite. He ran ahead of his family, looking, sniffing and generally checking everything out.*

*Deep in the woods he bounded around a corner and stopped in his tracks. There ahead of him, standing in the middle of the path, was a 250 pound black bear.*

*Under normal circumstances Frasier would have approached the newcomer or barked at it. This was not a normal circumstance. His instinct told him to turn around, get back to the pack, and warn them not to get any closer to the enormous hairy beast he had just discovered.*

*He succeeded in properly communicating the danger and his pack cautiously turned around and headed in the other direction. Frasier normally wasn't a fan of staying in hotels, but that night he made an exception.*

Sometimes at work we get to the point where we've done things so many times we just react instinctively. We rely on our experience to help us make quick decisions, and usually our gut is right.

The flip side of that is information myopia. We think we've encountered the identical situation before so we don't fully analyze all of the data. We quickly size up the matter and make a snap judgement.

Given how fast the world is changing, this can be a trap. In business you have to be ever alert to a shift in preferences or buying habits. Experience is a tremendous advantage but don't let it blind you to new data and ideas.

Top notch leaders never stop learning and gathering new information. They listen to webinars, attend tradeshows and read books from thought leaders. In a world where information is king, the best leaders help their team know more than the competition does. That's a real leg up.

- How much change do you expect in your business and how good are you and your organization at learning new things?
- In the past year, what new ideas have you tried?

## DOG WHISTLES

Dogs can hear things we can't. That's because our ears can only detect sounds up to twenty kilohertz while dogs can hear up to forty-five kilohertz.

When it comes to hearing, though, most human failings aren't because they can't hear their boss, customer or co-worker. It's because they aren't actively listening.

*George is a mutt. His mother is of Irish-German ancestry and grew up in Idaho, while his father is Greek by way of Texas. George has nice markings but his coat is thinning a little prematurely.*

*At work, George is the customer service manager for an electrical component distributor. He started his career on the phones, taking orders and handling customer complaints. After a few years in that role, someone ran a report to see how many customers continued to buy after having a complaint, and they filtered the results by the customer service rep who had taken the original call.*

*What they discovered was customers George handled were twice as likely to continue to be a customer versus the next best rep. When asked what his secret was, he said he listened hard. When he heard someone who was frustrated he empathized. Then he made things right.*

When we casually listen, we hear some of the words but miss the rest of the message. Active listening requires concentration. Processing every word, decoding clues in inflection, picking up on emotional tone and recapping key points. It takes a lot of work. But the net result is we actually *hear* what someone is saying.

Here are some tips on how to be a better listener:
- Have a genuine interest in what the other person is saying.
- Lock eyes with the speaker.
- Take notes.
- Ask questions to stay engaged and to dig deeper for a better understanding.
- Show empathy.
- Don't interrupt and let people finish their statements.
- Quiet the other thoughts that can race in your head and concentrate on the conversation.
- Repeat back key words that the other person said and emphasize the emotions. For example: "It must have been frustrating when the customer said he didn't want to meet with you."
- Add "Tell me more" and "And then what?" to your conversational vocabulary to drill down deeper into what the other person is saying.

Make sure everyone in the conversation feels heard whether you plan to implement their ideas or not. You'll have a greater chance of buy-in and consensus for the final solution because people will know their idea was considered with an open mind. And you'll probably generate better solutions. The game changing ideas may be outliers that are easily lost in the noise.

Seek input directly from your customers and front line workers. As a leader, the information you receive is typically filtered by your senior managers. While you should trust their judgement, nothing beats hearing directly from users and customer-facing co-workers.

Three-quarters of our waking hours are spent communicating with others. Of that nearly half is spent listening. We use listening skills more than speaking, reading and writing. Yet most people have never really learned how to listen. The next time you're about to tune out someone remember this: you'll never learn less by listening.

- How can you more actively listen for meaning rather than just for the words?
- How do you show the other person you are actively listening and interested in what they are saying?

# BARKS VS. WOOFS

Communication skills are vitally important in every workplace. Dogs have a limited vocabulary, but they are great communicators. Just as a bark doesn't convey the same meaning as a woof, so should you make sure you communicate effectively with each member of your team.

*Buddy, like most dogs, makes a lot of different sounds. He's a pretty good verbal communicator, although his diction needs a little work at times.*

*If he hears a faint sound from outside — say the sound of the mailman approaching — he makes a low, quiet growl. He's just letting the pack know he hears something.*

*When the mailman gets closer to the house, the quiet growl turns into a modest woof. No reason to get excited. Yet.*

*But when the mail slot opens and the assault begins — he gets particularly riled up by direct mail requests for political donations, for some reason — he leaps to his feet and lets out a series of barks that could turn a Republican into a Democrat.*

How you communicate with members of your team has a profound impact on your career. Try this: use the record voice app on your phone so you can hear how you sound. Is that how you want to come across? Most people don't think much about their tone of voice or delivery. Odds are you can boost your effectiveness by improving how you say things.

The most powerful aspect in communications — by a wide margin — is your body language. Next most significant is your tone of voice. And last on the list are the actual words you use. This may explain why dogs are so good at understanding what we say.

Your voice tone and modulations are critical because they convey a wide range of subliminal messages. Make sure yours communicates confidence and decisiveness, not nervousness and uncertainty.

Try to mirror the energy of the person with whom you are speaking. When you are talking with someone who is direct and decisive, speak in a clear, confident, bullet-pointed style. If you're interacting with a fun-loving and expressive person, speak in an enthusiastic, friendly, energetic style. Use a warm, soft and steady tone when speaking with someone who is calm, patient and logical. For analytical perfectionists, a controlled, thoughtful, measured tone is best.

When making key points you want to accentuate, make sure your voice inflections and pace reflect that importance. Varying your pitch and cadence can change the meaning of what you are saying. Of course, people can hear it when you smile, too.

Your voice is an important and often overlooked tool in your career. Make sure it shows you know what you're talking about, exudes confidence and conveys the appropriate emotions. After all, a bark isn't a woof or a growl.

- What does your tone of voice say to others?
- When you speak do you sound like a leader?

## YAPPERS

Look, the sun is up...*bark, bark, bark!* Hey, is there a squirrel in the tree? *Bark, bark, bark!* I think I heard something...*bark, bark, bark!* Someone is coming at you wearing a hockey mask while holding a machete...*bark, bark, bark!* My bad, it was just another squirrel...*bark, bark, bark!*

Some dogs love to talk. And talk. And talk. Most of the time they don't say very much.

Some people are like that. We say things just because we like to hear the sound of our own bark. Sometimes we feel the need to add to someone else's story or to jump into every discussion with our own two cents.

*A couple years ago we went to visit some out-of-town friends for the weekend. They convinced us to stay at their house, which sounded like a good idea.*

*They had a wonderful dog Rufus, a good-natured mix who loved everyone he met. That first night in their guest bedroom we discovered one of Rufus' other traits: he barked at every sound he heard. There was a car that drove by the house. Woof! The wind blew through the trees. Woof! The air conditioner kicked on. Woof!*

**Observant**

*We loved our friends, but by the next morning we realized we were not going to get any sleep in the same house as Rufus. So we checked into a hotel. We're all still friends today.*

If you've gotten as far as you have by being a great talker, congratulations. The question you have to ask is "Can I significantly advance my career without modifying how I come across?" We'll answer that for you: probably not.

Yappers come in many forms, but they have one thing in common: they waste time. There's the person who stops by your office and spends fifteen minutes talking about the football game you couldn't care less about. And there's the colleague who circle talks around a topic without ever saying anything.

When you talk too much, people tune you out. Be sure what you are going to say will add value to the conversation or help the person with whom you're speaking.

To avoid being perceived as a yapper, try to assess if the other person has time to talk. Perhaps they're under time pressure to complete a project, so it's best to check by asking "Is now a good time to talk?" If not, either schedule a time to have a deep dive conversation or be brief, be bright and be gone.

Circle talkers struggle to stay on topic or give succinct answers to questions. If that's you, work at getting to the point quickly. Focus on identifying the problem you are trying to solve and clearly laying out the rationale behind your recommendation.

If you work with a circle talker, stop them when they're rambling and say "Excuse me, I'm not following you. Can you tell me in three sentences the main points you are trying to make? That way I can wrap my head around it."

Don't dominate conversations, as it will come across as a power grab or ego trip. Be sure you've given everyone the opportunity to speak. And if you are with someone who is dominating the conversation, hold up your hand like a stop sign and say "I'd like others to contribute to the conversation. What does everyone else think?" You don't have to be rude but you may have to assertively interject.

Some other ideas to nip yapping co-workers are to stand up when a conversation runs long, set a time limit on how long each person can give an update in a team meeting and define the end of the conversation. "I have a hard stop in five minutes" is a great way to cut to the chase.

The good news for yappers is you don't have to completely change. In fact, that's impossible. You just need to temper your natural inclinations a little. If you know you like to talk, tell yourself every morning that today you will listen more, be curious about what the other person is saying and not be the first to jump into a conversation.

Better yet, become a great question *asker.* You'll win more friends and influence more people by asking *them* to tell you more. And then when you do have something to say, people will listen to your bark.

- What is your mix between asking good questions and listening attentively versus talking about yourself and your agenda?
- How can you be more intentional about what you and the other person should get out of a conversation?

## THE NOSE KNOWS

Dogs are very good at a lot of things, but when it comes to smelling, they are exceptional. Their ability to detect and decipher smells is significantly more acute than ours. They have fifty times more olfactory receptors in their noses and forty times more of their brain devoted to decoding the smell. No wonder they love hanging out in the kitchen.

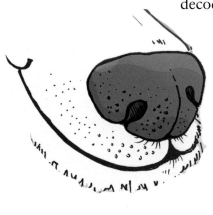

Unless you're in the fragrance industry or you clean up after fires for a living you probably don't think much about your sense of smell. We live in a visual world that's punctuated by sound and rounded out by taste.

And yet smell may be our most powerful sense in many ways. A whiff of cut grass, your old baseball glove or your mother's apple pie in the oven and you're transported back to a distant but vivid place. Can you find a way to evoke positive feelings for your company by tapping into the hidden power of smell?

*Maria is a pure bred. Her parents came to America from Mexico where they were descendants of Mayan rulers. At least that's what grandma always said.*

*Maria is the general manager at a large resort in Scottsdale. One day she received a box in the mail and opened it to discover samples of a new line of soap, shampoo and hand lotion. She was instantly struck by the wonderful scent of sandalwood, so she immediately washed her hands with the sample. It was absolutely heavenly.*

*She decided to try something new. She bought a small quantity of this new line of toiletries. When guests checked in they were offered samples to sniff: the original line and the new one. They got to choose which one they wanted.*

*Guest satisfaction increased by thirty-two percent.*

In the property restoration industry, eliminating smoke and moldy odors is an essential part of the business. In your industry, look for ways to add that new car smell experience to all of your existing products and services.

Some dogs have the ability to smell cancer, so don't underestimate your ability to sniff out problems. You'll likely smell the fire long before you see it, and your nose will detect your boss's perfume long before she makes it to your desk.

At work, you don't have to be a Bloodhound to be cognizant about how you smell. Breath mints and deodorants are widely available and a good idea. Also be careful about how much fragrance you wear to the office, as a little goes a long way.

The right scent can also have positive effects. Studies have shown that a small amount of peppermint oil can improve mental focus and boost creativity. So give your career that minty fresh smell and watch your productivity zoom.

As a leader, people look to you to sniff out lingering problems. And while that rarely involves using your olfactory lobe, it does require you to use all your senses. Including your intuition. When something doesn't smell right, you probably should investigate it further. Tap into your natural curiosity and follow your nose.

- How can you use your nose to detect opportunities?
- How can you try to sniff out potential problems?

*A hungry dog hunts best.*
– Lee Travino

## WALKING WITH THE PACK

Dogs exercise with gusto. They run, jump, spin, play, chase and generally go all out. It's fun for them, and because it's fun, they do it with enthusiasm.

We humans have a lot we can learn from our canine friends. Maybe not so much the spinning and jumping because we tend to get bad knees, but you get the idea. It's very easy to say we should exercise but a lot harder to do. The key to getting regular exercise is actually simple: you have to find something physical you enjoy doing and make it a habit.

*For us, after years of being weekend warriors when it comes to working out, we decided to try taking the dogs for a walk at 5:45 AM. We went as fast as we could without running, and with the hills in the area, it turned out we got our heartrates up pretty good, too. Even better, we all kind of liked it. So we did it again the next day. By the third morning our dogs were almost doing back flips when we put on our gym shoes.*

*Since then if we ever even think about blowing off the morning walk we get stares from our dogs that guilt us into getting off our duffs and going out for a walk. We can't say we like getting up early but we sure do love our pack time.*

It's a well-established fact that dogs live longer when they get plenty of exercise. And even the most die-hard couch potato knows that people who exercise regularly live longer, too. But perhaps even more importantly, our quality of life is improved. We have more energy at work. We look and

feel better. And we're more productive and innovative. We're better leaders.

You can get exercise in the office, too. Get up every hour and move around, even if only for a few minutes. Take the stairs instead of the elevator. Try having a "moving meeting" where you talk while you walk around the building instead of sitting in a conference room. Get a stand-up desk to improve your muscle tone, posture and metabolism.

Companies can foster self-improvement by creating an environment where employees feel the company really cares about them. We see it more and more today, driven in part by high medical costs and a competitive market for talent. Whatever is behind it, when companies actively help their associates improve their health it builds loyalty. And loyal colleagues work harder and with more passion. And that makes for happier, more loyal customers. Hmmm…sounds like a pretty good idea.

- What exercise are you doing on a daily basis?
- How can you incorporate more exercise into your daily work schedule?

## A BONE TO PICK

We are what we eat. Dogs are notoriously less finicky than humans when it comes to their diet. Offer them table scraps and they'll snarf it down, pronto.

*Bear and Molly, brother and sister Rhodesian Ridgebacks, are virtually omnivorous. They'll eat just about anything except fruits and vegetables. Unless it's a stew, in which case the carrots just taste like funky meat. Probably how we feel about tofu.*

*Bear is a little particular about what he eats, meaning he won't eat pineapple and artichokes. Molly, on the other hand, will eat anything. And by anything we mean everything. If it's on someone's dinner plate, she wants some. Did someone say ice cream? Two scoops, please!*

If you haven't already, consider upgrading what you consume. People everywhere are eating better, choosing higher quality, more natural food when they can.

Now don't get us wrong, you can still love your junk food. Just try to eat less of it. Drink more water, eat more salads and buy organic when available. And while your dogs may not be very discriminating when it comes to what they eat, you'll probably be happy you are.

And since this is a business leadership book, not a diet book, here's the point: if you eat smarter you will perform better at work. You will have more energy and you'll get more done. You'll win more customers and make them happier so they come back for more of whatever the heck it is you do. And all because you ate salads at lunch instead of large orders of bacon cheese fries.

In the canine world there are two kinds of eaters. The first are grazers who can have a bowl of food available to them to eat whenever they are hungry. When they are full, they stop. The second kind of dogs will devour an entire forty-pound bag of Kibbles 'n Bits if they can get their chops on it.

*Bailey is an Australian Shephard who belongs to a good friend of ours. A couple years ago they came over for dinner. At some point before dinner we — meaning the humans — got in the car to go somewhere for less than fifteen minutes, leaving our dogs and Bailey at home.*

*When we returned we found a mess. Our dogs are grazers. We fill the dog dish and they eat when they are hungry. It turns out Bailey is not a grazer.*

*When she realized there was a big dish full of interesting food, she went in head first. Technically it was mouth first, we think. All we know is when we returned a few minutes later, Bailey had devoured the entire bowl of food. And then, because she had eaten enough for two big dogs, she decided to throw it all up on the living room rug.*

*Dinner that night was slightly delayed.*

If you fall into the "clean plate" category you have a lot of company. This "say yes to everything" approach doesn't just apply to the food we eat. At work it can mean volunteering for every new project or accepting every request that comes our way. Saying yes makes the person asking pleased with us. Unfortunately, overcommitting can leave us overwhelmed, tired and stressed.

There are times when we need to say no — or at least not now — to things that aren't priorities. The more successful you are the more others will ask you to do things because they know your contribution will be an asset. While it's an honor to be asked to serve on a board or participate on other committees, if you are on too many it will sap your time and energy. It's a good idea to set boundaries on what you will and won't do…and eat.

- What changes should you make in what and how much you eat?
- What boundaries do you need to set and what do you need to say "no, not now" to?

## DOG BREATH

Having a sense of how you come across to others is critical for success. For example, you want to have enough self-awareness to know that you shed. And if you know you're a shedder, you shouldn't jump on a client's black velour sofa. That's the kind of self-awareness we're talking about here.

*A young couple in Birmingham, Tim and Gail, invited Gail's new boss Eleanor and her husband Kyle over for dinner. And while Eleanor and Kyle were delightful people, they were a bit more formal than their hosts.*

*As they all sat down to a bowl of homemade potato soup — in fact, just after Kyle said how much he loved vichyssoise — Rocky, Tim and Gail's two year old Vizsla, decided he needed to do some personal grooming. And by that we mean licking himself. Right there on the floor next to the guests at the dinner table. With gusto.*

*It's hard to say if that's what stalled Gail's upward mobility. Maybe Eleanor didn't like chilled soup.*

**Observant**

Having dog breath can be career-limiting. As much as we love our pooches, the unpleasant smell of a dog's panting is not terribly attractive. And while it's very difficult to get your dog to brush its teeth, it's actually pretty easy for humans to do it.

Exceptional leaders are self-aware about their strengths and weaknesses. They understand who they are and how their behaviors affect others. High self-awareness leads to better team performance and positively affects decision making and conflict management. Self-aware leaders are confident, know what goals they want to achieve and aren't afraid to learn how to improve. They also have a solid read of that other person in the room: their inner self.

Self-awareness helps you manage your emotions and understand how those feelings impact everyone around you. Here are some ways to improve:

- Make a list of your strengths and areas in need of improvement and look at it weekly.
- Notice throughout the day how you're feeling emotionally and energy-wise and how that correlates to the way you interact with others.
- Ask for feedback from friends and family about how you come across to others.
- Take a behavior or emotional intelligence assessment or have someone conduct a 360 survey about you.
- Write down your priorities, assess why they are important to you and determine if your behaviors and priorities are aligned.
- Ask yourself "What am I trying to achieve?" "What is working and what is not working yet?" "What should I change?"
- Meditate to improve your in-the-moment awareness.

In life it's the little things that often matter most. Don't let blind spots hold you back from your full leadership potential. When you ask for help in knowing what everyone else sees about you, you build open relationships and credibility which will increase your leadership effectiveness. And by practicing self-awareness you'll create an organization that learns, innovates and adapts faster to change.

- What are your strengths and what areas do you need to improve?
- What internal feedback techniques can you add to self-assess how you come across?

## DO YOU SEE WHAT I SEE?

Many people think dogs can't see as well as we can. It's true they can't see as many colors as humans do, but they make up for it in other ways. They can see better in low light at night, they detect motion faster and they have better peripheral vision. Let's just call this one a draw.

Dogs use their visual acuity differently than we do by focusing on things more intensely.

*Echo is a bird dog. Technically he's a Pointer but that's just for his papers.*

*Echo lives in Albany, Georgia. On weekends he goes hunting with his human friend. Echo loves to find quail. And he's really good at it.*

*As they walk through the long grasses he keeps his eyes peeled for any movement. When he spots a bird he freezes, body pointed directly at the bird. He's not crazy about the loud noises, but his human friend always praises Echo, which makes him very happy.*

At work, most people don't think much about their sense of vision unless they can't find their reading glasses. There is a mountain of visual information out there in body language. You just have to look for it. When shown a sheet of white paper with a single black dot on it, most people say they see a black dot. But there is so much more white space to see.

When your dog stands next to the door it's a signal that it has to go out. But you'll only see that if you're looking for it. Sometimes you have to push yourself to see things differently at work, too. It helps to change your perspective, like putting yourself in your customer's shoes so you can see the world through their eyes. A change in angle may help you look at your product the way a new prospect sees it for the first time.

Don't let your brain filter out what is too familiar or get locked in on your first impression. Look at the whole picture, not just what you think is most important. Like looking at a *Where's Waldo?* image, the thing you're looking for may be hiding in plain sight. And at the end of this reexamination you may realize it's time to enforce that uniform policy for your frontline workers or clean up your office so prospects get the right first impression.

Even though we don't actually see in black and white, many of us think that way. Things are good or bad, right or wrong. This binary way of approaching life can help you be more decisive, but it blinds you to the myriad of colors that exist. Open your eyes to the full spectrum and you'll discover new ways to innovate and expand your business.

A laser sharp focus is a keen asset for any leader, but there are times when you need to take a lesson from a dog and broaden your view. Your next business threat may not come from your known competitors, so expand your horizons. Airlines have learned how to speed up the turnaround time for flights by watching Indy 500 pit crews in action. Look at other industries for innovative ideas that can be applied to your business to gain a competitive advantage or make you more operationally efficient. Broaden your view of the world and see how high your team can fly.

- Are you looking at things in black and white or are you noticing the nuances of full color?
- Where should you look for innovative ideas to make your business more efficient or customer friendly?

## EVERY MUTT'S CRAZY 'BOUT A SHARP DRESSED LAB

Dogs rely on their family members to brush them and keep them well groomed. We live in an image conscious world, so it can be important for us to look good at work, too.

Have you ever seen the look a Boxer gives a Poodle who just got back from the groomer with balls on his feet and poofs all over his head and tail? Probably not. Dogs don't pay much attention to that stuff.

*We've never given our Standard Poodles the traditional Poodle haircut. We just tell the groomer "same length all over" and they come out looking like, well, most other dogs.*

*Except one time. We had gone to a new groomer. Despite giving the unambiguous "same length" sermon, when we picked up our dog he had a ball on his tail and poofy feet. We were in a hurry, so we figured we'd just trim him up when we got home and we left.*

*The problem was he didn't like getting groomed. So after we went at him with a pair of scissors for an hour to no avail we finally gave up. He was going to be a seventy-five pound white foo-foo Poodle for the next two months, like it or not.*

How you look and dress are key components of making a good leadership impression and speak volumes about you as a professional. Your appearance should help you connect with people, not create a barrier. You want your attire to inspire confidence in everyone you encounter.

As you get dressed in the morning, think about what the people you'll be with will be wearing. It's true that when you look good you'll feel confident and ready to work. If possible, dress in a way that you wouldn't be embarrassed to go to lunch with anyone at any restaurant in town.

Your executive presence creates your personal brand. Your personal brand is the image that comes to mind when people think about you. Your style, physical appearance and even the look of your workplace are all woven together — consciously or subconsciously — into this entity others call *you*.

Here's the real point: be aware of your own grooming. Gentlemen, shave every once in a while, take a shower and use some deodorant. Your co-workers will thank you. Ladies, don't dress for work like you're going on a hot date. And if you're really interested in upward mobility, pay close attention to the leaders in your organization and their grooming, manners and executive presence.

- What does your appearance communicate about you as a leader?
- What can you do to improve your professional appearance?

## THE COMMUNICATIONS GAP

Leaders are to their co-workers what people who have dogs are to their pets. Good management produces a happy, motivated and loyal team. Dogs that live with people who love and care for them while maintaining discipline and structure are generally the best adapted to the modern world.

The phrase "treat them like a dog" gets in the way of this analogy, because if you really do, you'll treat co-workers like a member of the family, with love and respect.

Dogs are always looking for information. They watch to see if you are packing a suitcase as an indication of an upcoming trip. They sniff your clothes to figure out where you've been. They listen for the sounds of someone approaching the front door.

*Coco is a Miniature Pinscher who's not quite tall enough to look out the windows in the front of her house. So she has to rely on her other senses to detect what's going on in the neighborhood. Like a radio telescope listening to the cosmos for signs of extraterrestrial life, Coco listens to every sound her highly sensitive ears can pick up. So far the closest she's come to a breakthrough discovery was a drone the boy next door flew into the side of her house.*

*Coco's family members don't possess her well-developed sense of hearing. Which is why they attached a bell on a string to the back door. That way when she needs to go out, all she has to do is bat the bell with her paw. And hope the boy next door isn't launching his ear-shattering model rocket at the same time.*

Employees are similar. They want more information from their bosses about what is going on and how they are doing. In the absence of clear and open communications from management, they will turn up their sensors to detect signals in the workplace. Companies that develop an open dialogue with their associates will reap the reward of having energy focused on the most important things — like exceeding customer satisfaction — instead of on rumors and misinformation.

You need to paint the picture so your team can clearly see what success looks like. Get used to adding the phrase "What I mean by that is…" as it forces you to be specific. And if someone is not clear with you, ask:

- "Help me to understand that better."
- "What do you mean by that?"
- "If this was a video, what would it look like? Can you help me visualize it?"

Here are some ways to improve communications at your organization:
- Host a brief department or company-wide gathering on a regular basis to keep everyone in the loop on what's happening within the company.
- Hold a daily five minute stand-up huddle with your core team. Have each person give a brief update on what they accomplished the previous day, what they plan to do that day and what they need from other team members.
- Create dedicated spaces within your workplace to encourage collaboration.
- Initiate an on-boarding process for all new employees so everyone understands the organization, it's vision and priorities.
- Make cascading communications throughout your organization a priority. At the end of leadership meetings, decide what messages should be shared and then each person disseminates that information with their team and ultimately with the rest of the organization.
- Use collaboration technology.

Too often we say things that can have different meanings to different people. Phrases like "take it to the next level" or "great job" are fine if they are further clarified. As a leader it is important to be specific about what a higher level of performance looks like or exactly what behaviors need to be exhibited to accomplish the goal.

- How do you ensure everyone within your organization has the information they need to succeed?
- What do you need to do to make the content of your communications more clear, specific and understood by all?

## LOOSE LEASH
The loose leash approach works well when managing employees who know what they are doing and what the goals are. It's for those who have delivered good results in the past and have

self-discipline, self-confidence and motivation. With these circumstances you can give them a long leash, meaning you don't need to hover over them and get daily reports.

*Wolfgang is a mutt who appears to be a combination of Whippet, Border Collie and Albert Einstein. His family in Glen Ellyn, Illinois thinks he's the smartest dog they've ever had. That's because Wolfgang understands almost everything he hears. Although when they discuss the Electoral College he usually cocks his head as if to say "So you mean we don't actually vote for the President?"*

*Anyway, he gets most things. And he is typically well behaved. So when they all go for a walk, Wolfgang gets the loose leash. His family hooks it on to his collar and away they go. Sure, sometimes he pulls, but generally speaking, he knows how fast they go. And when he sees a tree that he needs to mark, he's got enough leeway to take care of business.*

The key is making sure your colleagues know you are giving them a lot of freedom because they have earned it. They've performed in the past. They're performing now. And you are confident in their ability to perform in the future. They are well trained and have the experience and skill sets to do the job. When it is appropriate, loose leash associates will deliver better results and improved creativity than if they were managed differently.

Delegating is difficult for many managers, and yet it is one of your most powerful tools, especially with loose leash partners. Proper delegation is your way to empower the right people and buy more time for you.

Most managers don't delegate because it initially takes longer than doing it yourself and it means giving up control. Decide what the best use of your time is: staying in the weeds or investing time to teach someone else who can own the project moving forward. If it's a reoccurring task that would help the other person grow, delegate it.

In order for delegating to be successful, you need to coach. Show them how and emphasize why they are to do something a certain way. Be there to support them but allow them to fail so they can learn.

You can delegate responsibility and authority, but you can't delegate accountability. As the leader you still own the success or failure of your team's project. Luckily, most loose leash employees, with proper support and reinforcement, are ideally suited to take on delegated responsibilities.

A long leash is great for those experienced high-performers. But if you manage new or inexperienced associates with a long leash, problems can follow. Take the new hire who is simply told to "go learn it and we'll talk later." They can feel abandoned and ignored as they struggle to figure out the duties, expectations and culture of a new company.

- Do you adjust your leash length based on the person's ability to deliver results or do you have a one size fits all approach?
- Which associates would produce better results if you gave them a longer leash?

## SHORT LEASH

The other end of the spectrum — a short leash — is a good strategy for associates who have not earned the extra freedom a loose leash affords. Maybe it's because they're new, or perhaps they've made some mistakes. Whatever the reason, as a manager, you need to keep close tabs on these associates.

*Ginger is an eight-pound black and white pooch with undeterminable ancestry and a tendency to unleash a barking barrage with the slightest provocation. This is not her most admirable quality.*

*Never is this more evident than when she sees another dog on the street. Ginger's first inclination is to run over and say "hi," followed by a quick game of "let's bat at each other, growl a little and get down to some serious sniffing." This isn't always well received.*

*So now when her family sees another dog approaching on a walk, they adopt the short leash. It's like in baseball when you have two strikes and you choke up on the bat. Only in this case it's the leash.*

*And it works. It sends the very clear message to Ginger that she does not have as much room to maneuver. And that lunging at the oncoming Pit Bull may not be the smartest move.*

*She's starting to get the message.*

There are also situations where a short leash is needed even for proven performers. For example, when working on a critical time-sensitive project, the leader has to be certain everyone is and remains aligned. And the only way to ensure that may be with detailed daily updates.

Experienced, high-performers will chafe at a short leash under normal circumstances. They'll view micromanaging as demeaning and controlling. Few things will kill enthusiasm faster among your rainmakers than putting them on a short leash.

A short leash will make a new employee feel like they are getting the attention they need to learn quickly. When they prove their abilities, loosen the leash and give them increasingly more difficult tasks as you get comfortable with their performance. Be clear about your expectations, especially how and how often you want to be kept informed about progress. A simple weekly progress email — describing what was accomplished in the past week, what will be accomplished the next week and what they need from you — may be all that's needed.

We all know managers who keep everything on a short leash. They're the ones who want to be copied on all emails, check in on projects too often and who review expense reports like they're backpacks of workers at diamond mines. Their team typically feels a lack of trust because they micromanage everyone and every detail.

Attention to detail is a good thing, but a leash that's too short can lead to a culture of fear. If you're staying in the weeds, you're not likely to be doing the higher level work you should be doing for your job.

If you are a manager who spends too much time in the weeds, here are some ways you can change:
- Eliminate non-essential activities and delegate what you can.
- Don't spend time on anything below a specific numeric or dollar threshold.
- Refocus your efforts on those parts of your business that contribute to the bottom line.
- Concentrate on getting more efficient and improving KPIs.
- Refrain from constantly asking how it's going and when something will be done. Instead, establish agreed upon checkpoints for review, like at weekly one-on-one meetings or when the project is 25%, 50% or 75% complete.

It's a calculated balance between giving enough leash for your team to best use their abilities while still monitoring progress and supporting efforts to ensure successful outcomes.

- What are you doing on a regular basis that you can stop doing or delegate?
- What associates would produce better results if they were on a shorter leash?

## INVISIBLE FENCE

Ah, the wonders of modern technology. With the invisible fence method of management, the team member has the feeling of freedom combined with an electronic monitoring system to ensure compliance.

*Lucky is an Australian Terrier who lives in the city. His home includes a modest backyard and a busy street out front. Given the way the driveway fits into the property, fencing in the backyard isn't a good option.*

*Enter the invisible fence. To be clear, Lucky initially wasn't a big fan of wearing a collar that had the ability to produce electric shocks. But once he understood how it worked and how to avoid the dreaded "slight corrections," he discovered the beauty of virtual freedom.*

*Now he can go out and survey his kingdom in total privacy. All he has to do is paw at the back door to let everyone know when he's ready to come back inside.*

Examples of the invisible fence style of management are work-from-home partners who need to process a certain number of jobs per day or generate sales calls, all without any direct supervision. As long as the work gets done properly, it's okay that they are sitting in their kitchen working on Wi-Fi. Caution: if you go too far from your house you might get a slight — zap! — correction.

Working remotely without a physical fence has plenty of plusses and minuses. On the upside, people can live and work anywhere and manage flexible schedules. The downside of having remote employees can manifest as challenges forming bonds within the team and difficulty staying connected on projects. Fortunately there are dozens of new technologies to help bring the team together even when remote.

The key here for leaders is to make extra efforts to build powerful connections between remote team members and those in the office. It's important to set clear expectations and no matter how remote the partner is, make the effort to visit them or bring them in so you can meet face-to-face on a regular basis.

- What new technologies could help you improve productivity and increase collaboration?
- When can your team work productively from home?

## WHO LET THE DOGS OUT

It used to be dogs were outdoor pets. Today, the thought of having a dog that lives outdoors is kind of crazy to many people, but it's a viable option for some dogs that are well suited to the elements.

*King is a Husky mix who lives forty miles east of Denver. He likes to explore, and he has lots of room in his fenced in yard to do just that. Sometimes, in the course of his ventures, he does a little digging. Okay, he actually digs a lot.*

*He likes being an outdoor dog. It gives him the freedom to do as he pleases. There's always food and water, and a place on the porch to get out of the rain. On those nights when it gets a little too cold, he gets invited inside the house.*

*He wouldn't have it any other way.*

In the business world, there are some salespeople who are invaluable in the field. They love meeting customers and traveling from city to city, drumming up work. Put them in a cubicle for a day and they go nuts. As a manager you have to assess the business need and the individual's disposition before deciding if they have what it takes to be an "outdoor dog."

Or let's say you are managing a former business owner who lives two time zones away and is exploring a new market for your company. How you manage that individual should be very different from how you manage a new hire in your data entry department.

Never forget the real world is outside your corporate headquarters' four walls. That's where your customers live, so get out and see them. Watch them use your products and services, find out what matters most to them and get the kind of unfiltered feedback you need to make good decisions. You also will learn a lot about your own offices and what's really happening in the field.

Fences create places where dogs have freedom to roam. At work there are virtual fences between departments that can prevent people from exchanging vital information. Make sure the fences in your business are there to create clear expectations without limiting innovation and growth.

Great leaders are outdoor dogs who know how to speak with indoor voices.

- What fences need to come down so people can better collaborate?
- How could your business grow with more people out in the field seeing customers and observing market trends?

# Observant

**Observant leaders are:**
- Perceptive
- Aware
- Curious

**Observant leaders succeed because they:**
- Are always looking for more information.
- Ask meaningful questions.
- Spot problems earlier by paying attention to details others don't see.
- Use their senses, watch for body language and listen for tone to understand the true meaning of a message.
- Delegate to help others grow and to get more done.
- See opportunities to innovate and be more efficient.
- Adjust their leadership style based on the other person's needs.
- Get out and meet customers to learn what's really going on.
- Ensure people have the information they need to succeed.

**Observant leaders are respected because they:**
- Don't dominate conversations.
- Communicate consistently with tone of voice and body language in addition to words.
- Actively listen and don't interrupt.
- Broaden their view and change their perspective so they see new things.
- Are emotionally intelligent.
- Have executive presence.
- Work on areas they need to improve.
- Are self-aware of their behaviors and their impact on others.

*Be the person your dog thinks you are.*
– J.W. Stephens

# The Doghouse

Most people have a desire to succeed at work. On a personal level they want to become well respected, advance in their careers and make more money. On an organizational level they want to lead, help their team succeed and be a valuable partner for customers. These are all noble and positive inclinations.

For all their wonderful traits, we'd be making a big mistake if we always acted like a dog at work. Remember that desire to earn respect and move up the corporate food chain? If you go overboard on this dog thing you can forget about it.

You probably know this already, but just to make sure, here are some dogisms that will put you in the doghouse wearing the cone of shame.

## HUMPING

Few things will get you in bigger trouble faster than humping at work. It's a surefire way to derail your career and ruin your reputation. Dogs don't have the same social norms that humans have, so you'll be well advised not to take this whole "doggy style" thing too far while on the job.

## LICKING

Using your tongue to seal an envelope is okay at work, but that's about it in the licking department. Especially off limits is the kind of personal grooming that dogs are famous for. Not only is it much harder for people to do for basic physiological reasons, it's especially awkward to do it in a cubicle. And if the boss catches you in the middle of it, you can lick your career goodbye.

## BARKING

If you have a dog that barks at everything, to the point of driving everyone bonkers, you have some options. One is to put the dog outside (or bring them in). You can try to distract it with a toy. Or you can do what most people do, which is threaten to eliminate *Animal Planet* from your favorites on your TV's remote control if it doesn't shut up.

There are some people who are loud at work, and if that is distracting to others, you need to talk with them about using their "inside bark" at work.

## SNIFFING

Dogs have an amazing sense of smell, and they use it to learn more about whoever they encounter. Humans, on the other hand, don't have a particularly great sense of smell, so it is advisable to keep your nose out of other people's personal business unless you're asked.

## DOG FIGHTING

Dogs can look like they're fighting even when they're playing. When threatened, they're not averse to settling the score with a knock-down, drag out brawl. The workplace, however, is not a good place to demonstrate mixed martial arts on a co-worker, and aggressive fighting with a customer is one of the surest ways to get permanently uninvited back to the office. Don't be so dominant that you are constantly looking to pick fights.

## MUDDY PAWS

For thousands of years, dogs lived outside. They ran around in the wild and no one was upset because they tracked a little mud in the cave. The world has changed. Now our corporate caves have plush carpeting and the company logo inlaid in tile in the lobby. And the facilities people really hate it when we track mud on the company logo.

Of course, this obsession with clean workplaces extends to desks, offices and vehicles where germs can be transmitted. A word to the wise: wipe your paws.

## BITCH

While "bitch" is a perfectly legitimate word, our advice is to just say "female dog" and avoid the funny looks. Its far more common usage, of course, is as a synonym for bellyache. We all know people — men and women — who complain about everything. The coffee stinks, the room's too cold, the parking lot has potholes...everything seems to annoy them. And they feel compelled to share their displeasure with everyone.

If you have a tendency to whine, curb it. You're annoying the heck out of your co-workers and limiting your career path.

## FALSE ALARMS

Given their predilection for keeping the pack safe, dogs tend to alert us when they sense danger. And in their world, that may mean hearing children walking down the street and mistakenly thinking they're an invading hoard with axes, torches and chainsaws. In these circumstances, dogs bark and snarl and generally have a conniption fit. For about fifteen seconds. Then they fall back to sleep.

While we all appreciate the value of a canary in a coal mine, no one likes it when the false alarm is sounded over and over causing unnecessary stress.

## SCOOP UP THE MESS

Unless it involves food, dogs are notoriously weak at cleaning up after themselves. Workplaces shouldn't resemble the den of a cackle of hyenas, so get rid of the clutter. Eliminate stacks of paper by taking action on the critical documents, filing away the ones you need to save and throwing out the rest. Fair or not, many people consider a messy desk a sign of laziness. So scoop up your mess.

## DRINKING FROM THE TOILET

When thirsty, dogs will drink out of almost anything. If they drink from a toilet they can catch some nasty germs. Having a drink with a customer or co-worker can be a great way to bond, but if you aren't careful it can lead to problems. Make sure you don't jeopardize your career with ill-advised drinking habits.

- What career-limiting behaviors do you need to stop?
- With whom do you need to discuss career-limiting behaviors to help that coworker avoid the doghouse?

*Some dog I've got, too. We call him Egypt.*
*Because in every room he leaves a pyramid.*
– Rodney Dangerfield

# The Tail End

The bond between people and dogs is powerful. They're crazy about us and we love the fur out of them. And it isn't just because they are faithful, inspirational, determined and observant. We just like spending time together.

But the truth is our relationship goes much deeper than that. Dogs are our best friends. We play together, laugh together, eat together and explore together. Few things in life are as pure as the love of a dog.

As you reflect on the leadership impact you want to have, some things are a given. You want your teammates to say you brought out their best, achieved results, motivated them and picked up on important details. The real question is this: *are you the leader your dog would be proud of?*

You don't get to decide whether you're a leader or not. That's the job of the pack. They listen to how you speak, watch how you behave and measure your results.

The good news is you control your attitudes and actions, and they ultimately determine your leadership brand. You decide what you say and what you do. When you continue to do everything within your power to improve yourself, you — like every dog — will have your day. And maybe your own corner office.

This is the tail end of the book. By now we all know that dogs are a fountainhead of leadership wisdom. The real challenge is putting these doggone great ideas into meaningful business action.

Becoming a better leader isn't easy. You'll have to work hard and get your paws dirty. If you're willing to focus on *The Fido Factor*, you'll get a leg up at work.

*Every dog must have its day.*
– Jonathan Swift

# The Fido Factor Online

Please visit **www.TheFidoFactor.com** to explore more and take a deeper dive into the intersection of leadership, business and four-legged friends.

Share your photos, videos and stories on **The Fido Factor Blog**. We want to hear from you about the leadership lessons you've learned from your dog and examples of the Fido Factor in action.

**The Fido Factor Assessment Tool** is free and can help you maximize your leadership potential. It's fast and easy. After a few clicks of the mouse you'll know your personal Fido Factor score.

Discover the other resources and tools at **The Fido Factor Resource Guide**. This includes links to other helpful websites and Fido Factor tools you can put to use today. We have met many incredible people, companies and dogs along this journey. This is our opportunity to share what we've learned with you.

And don't forget to follow **The Fido Factor** on social media!

# Acknowledgements

We owe a big bark out to all of our friends and associates who helped us make *The Fido Factor* what it is. We couldn't have done it without you...thank you!

Extra special thanks to Gerry Pasqualetti (illustrations), Judy McDonough at PR By The Book (public relations), Jill Bridges at Optimized Scribes (social media marketing), Sarah McArthur (editing), Jill Nilsen (editing), Stephen Sullivan (design/layout), Gerry Pasqualetti (design/layout), Reversed Out (website), Debra Shepard (photography), Andy Barr (insight), Barbara & Roderick Barr (encouragement), Irmgard & Horst Hehmann (wisdom) and Rod Barr (structure).

Also, special thanks to everyone who read drafts of the book and helped steer us in the right direction, including Robin Klayman, Dr. Bob Biederman, Dave Peck, Jim Pancero, Scott Farmer, Jack Roehr, Steve Olberding, Steve Dilbone, Scott Gregory, Matt Lorenz, Lee Ann Kiefer, Tim Pappas, Sue McElroy, Bob Capobianco, Tony Kuczinski, Steve Black, Lisa Hillenbrand, Heide Moser, Diane Stevens, Elaine Riggins, Don Brown, Matt Scherocman, Carol Gaffney, Mark Faust, Catherine Vernon, Nancy Lynch, Glenda Lamont, David Rosenthal, Ron Campbell, Adam Koehler, Chris Moore, Michelle Taute, Bob Kissel, Adriana Llames, Lisa LaFata Powell, Sophie Swarthout, Eric Eiselt, Sherry Kearns, Shelly Wallace and Carolee Langhorne.

# The Authors

**Krissi Barr** is founder and CEO of Barr Corporate Success, a business consulting company. Her firm specializes in strategic planning and implementation, executive coaching, training, and behavioral assessments. Krissi is an accomplished public speaker and one of the most dynamic business leaders in America today. For more information please visit www.krissibarr.com.

**Dan Barr** is an accomplished sales and marketing leader, having delivered results at BELFOR Property Restoration's 1-800 WATER DAMAGE brand, Cintas and his own businesses.

The Barrs live in Cincinnati with their two dogs, Kaiser and Clover. *The Fido Factor: How to Get a Leg Up at Work* is their second book. Their first was *Plugged: Dig Out and Get the Right Things Done*, a business book with a golf theme.

*A portion of the proceeds from this book will be donated to canine charities.*